WILLIAM WYCHERLEY

The Country Wife

Edited by

THOMAS H. FUJIMURA

University of Nebraska Press
Lincoln and London

REGENTS RESTORATION DRAMA SERIES

General Editor: John Loftis

THE COUNTRY WIFE

Regents Restoration Drama Series

The Regents Restoration Drama Series, similar in objectives and format to the Regents Renaissance Drama Series, will provide soundly edited texts, in modern spelling, of the more significant English plays of the late seventeenth and early eighteenth centuries. The word "Restoration" is here used ambiguously and must be explained. If to the historian it refers to the period between 1660 and 1685 (or 1688), it has long been used by the student of drama in default of a more precise word to refer to plays belonging to the dramatic tradition established in the 1660's, weakening after 1700, and displaced in the 1730's. It is in ,this extended sense—imprecise though justified by academic custom—that the word is used in this series, which will include plays first produced between 1660 and 1737. Although these limiting dates are determined by political events, the return of Charles II (and the removal of prohibitions against the operation of theaters) and the passage of Walpole's Stage Licensing Act, they enclose a period of dramatic history having a coherence of its own in the establishment, development, and disintegration of a tradition.

Each text in the series is based on a fresh collation of the seventeenth- and eighteenth-century editions that might be presumed to have authority. The textual notes, which appear above the rule at the bottom of each page, record all substantive departures from the edition used as the copy-text. Variant substantive readings among contemporary editions are listed there as well. Editions later than the eighteenth century are referred to in the textual notes only when an emendation originating in some one of them is received into the text. Variants of accidentals (spelling, punctuation, capitalization) are not recorded in the notes. Contracted forms of characters' names are silently expanded in speech prefixes and stage directions, and, in the case of speech prefixes, are regularized. Additions to the stage directions of the copy-text are enclosed in brackets. Stage directions such as "within" or "aside" are enclosed in parentheses when they occur in the copy-text.

Spelling has been modernized along consciously conservative lines, but within the limits of a modernized text the linguistic quality of the original has been carefully preserved. Punctuation has been brought into accord with modern practices. The objective has been to achieve a balance between the generally light pointing of the old editions, and a system of punctuation which, without overloading the text with exclamation marks, semicolons, and dashes, will make the often loosely flowing verse and prose of the original syntactically intelligible to the modern reader. Dashes are regularly used only to indicate interrupted speeches, or shifts of address within a single speech.

Explanatory notes, chiefly concerned with glossing obsolete words and phrases, are printed below the textual notes at the bottom of each page. References to stage directions in the notes follow the admirable system of the Revels editions, whereby stage directions are keyed, decimally, to the line of the text before or after which they occur. Thus, a note on 0.2 has reference to the second line of the stage direction at the beginning of the scene in question. A note on 115.1 has reference to the first line of the stage direction following line 115 of the text of the relevant scene. Speech prefixes, and any stage directions attached to them, are keyed to the first line of accompanying dialogue.

JOHN LOFTIS

Stanford University

Contents

Abbreviations

Introduction

The Country Wife is William Wycherley's third comedy and his best. It is entered in the Stationers' Register for January 13, 1674/75, and in the Term Catalogues for May, 1675. The first edition, a quarto dated 1675, is the only authoritative text; it is highly reliable, and it has been used as the copy-text for the present modernized edition, into which some corrected readings from later editions have been introduced. Four more quartos of the play appeared during Wycherley's lifetime, but it appears unlikely that he could have revised them. The second quarto, of 1683, introduces a few corrections; but since Wycherley was then in prison, these were probably not made by him. The third quarto, of 1688, a paginal reprint of the 1683 edition, shows some deterioration. The fourth quarto, of 1695, is reprinted from the 1683 text, which it follows pretty faithfully; it came out during Wycherley's temporary retirement to Clive. The fifth quarto, also published in 1695, is a paginal reprint of the fourth; it appears to have been hastily printed, for it introduces many changes, and it omits and transposes words.[1] In 1713, Wycherley's plays were published in octavo under the title, *The Works of the Ingenious Mr. W. W. Collected Into One Volume*. The 1713 text of *The Country Wife*, which is based on the fourth quarto, is an unusually good one; it even incorporates from earlier quartos a few readings better than those in the fourth. Yet it appears unlikely that the old and ailing author could have had much to do with this edition.

The exact date of the first performance of *The Country Wife* is unknown. The Lord Chamberlain's records in the Public Record Office indicate that it was acted before royalty at the Theatre Royal

[1] Quartos four and five are reversed in Gertrude L. Woodward and James G. McManaway, *A Check List of English Plays 1641–1700* (Chicago, 1945), p. 145: Q4, with *Country-Wife* in the running title, is listed as item 1326; Q5, with *Country Wife* in the running title, is item 1325. For an account of the two 1695 quartos, see Robert N. E. Megaw, "The Two 1695 Editions of Wycherley's *Country-Wife*," *Studies in Bibliography*, III (1950–1951), 252–253. Megaw derives Q4 from the 1688 edition, but collation shows that it is based on the 1683 edition.

in Drury Lane on January 12 and again on January 15, 1674/75.[2] Though 1675 thus seems the earliest date, the prologue apparently refers to a performance not long after the relative failure of an earlier play, possibly *The Gentleman Dancing-Master* produced in 1672. But the phrase in the prologue, "the late so baffled scribbler of this day," is too vague to be meaningful. *The Country Wife* was a great success in 1675, with Horner played by the veteran actor Charles Hart, who was supported by a strong cast of experienced actors. It maintained its popularity through the first half of the next century; but the increasingly moral tone of the audience led to an adaptation of the play by David Garrick. This version, titled *The Country Girl* (1766), supplanted the original version till the twentieth century.[3]

The Country Wife is the purest expression of Wycherley's dramatic genius. Though the idea for Horner's pretended impotence is taken from Terence's *Eunuchus*, and some scenes are indebted to Molière's *L'École des Maris* and also *L'École des Femmes*, the play is Wycherley's own, and deserves its high reputation.[4] His best play, it is superior in almost every respect to his other three comedies, *Love in a Wood* (1671), *The Gentleman Dancing-Master* (1672), and even *The Plain Dealer* (1676). *The Country Wife* surpasses these in structure, in dramatic situations, characterization, comic dialogue, and in satiric wit and irony. Though some may prefer *The Plain Dealer* for its more caustic satire and for its character of Manly, *The Country Wife* must be judged superior as a dramatic piece.

Structurally, the play has more unity than most comedies of the Restoration. To be sure, there are three strands to the plot, and one of these, the Harcourt-Alithea story, is rather slight; but the three are linked, not only through Margery Pinchwife, but thematically. The result is a clear dramatic line which, despite complications, creates no confusion on the stage: not only do the three strands neatly mesh from act to act, but they provide effective counterpoint to each other. Thus, the three men (Horner, Pinchwife, and Harcourt) are as formally contrasted as the three women (Margery, Lady Fidget, and

---

[2] Allardyce Nicoll, *A History of English Drama*, I (Cambridge, 1952), 345, 439.

[3] For the stage history of the play, see Emmett L. Avery, "*The Country Wife* in the Eighteenth Century," *Research Studies of the State College of Washington*, X (1942), 142–158.

[4] John Wilcox, *The Relation of Molière to Restoration Comedy* (New York, 1938), pp. 87–94.

Alithea); and their responses to marriage and sex not only shape the plot but elucidate the theme. Superficially, the comic plot involves situations common to Restoration comedies; that is, outwitting or exposure, with the more-intelligent defeating those who are less clever or less honest. But the dramatic intent goes beyond mere outwitting. The Horner-Fidget story and the Pinchwife story, which parallel each other, are set off against the Harcourt-Alithea-Sparkish story. The result is a neat play, excelling in structure most Restoration comedies.

At the same time, the clarity and unity of the dramatic action should not obscure the fact that the plot is often close to farce. Though clearly delineated, the action borders on the improbable, particularly with Horner's intrigue and his involvement with Margery. The pretense of impotence by Horner is a dramatic premise upon which the remainder of the main action is based; a willing suspension of disbelief is thus called for at the very beginning. Yet, however improbable the assumption, it gives Wycherley an opportunity to exploit the dramatic possibilities of secrecy, disclosure, and mistakes incident to such a ruse. The basic comic idea lends itself to dramatic irony; for the contrast between appearance and reality sets up those situations that make for irony. These situations are then exploited fully, without subtlety or restraint. The individual scenes are striking, often farcical, and bitingly satirical. The gullibility of Sir Jasper Fidget and the folly of Pinchwife are stripped bare on the stage; and the comic victims are lashed by the satirist without mercy. Wycherley's play is not for the squeamish or dainty. But if a play is to be judged for its effectiveness on the stage, through its integration of character, theme, and plot, *The Country Wife* is indeed a superior comedy.

Some may object to the play because of its subject or its moral tone, particularly in the notorious "china" scene. Since sex is a main ingredient, we need to look at the central symbol who dominates the play. Horner, as his name implies, is a maker of cuckolds, a predatory gallant who seems to stalk all women within his purlieu. Yet he has a far more complex role than is suggested by his name. In one sense, he is that instrument of Wycherley's who, by putting on the appearance of impotence, effectively exposes other affecters of appearance. He is also the means by which the foolish Pinchwife and other stupid husbands are punished. Thus Horner is a kind of *deus ex machina* for the author's satiric exploitation of unworthy characters. Beyond this,

Horner is a respectable figure, though by no means a paragon of the Restoration rake. Of his intrigue, it should be pointed out that the goal is simply access to lustful women who bar the way with a pretense to virtue. In the play, Horner's "victims" are predatory libertines like Lady Fidget or aggressive wives like Margery; he makes no advances to the virtuous Alithea, nor shows any inclination to outwit Harcourt for her favors. Indeed, Horner is genuinely concerned at one point over his friend's seeming loss of Alithea.

More important, Horner's activities transcend mere libertinism; he is motivated by a desire to expose hypocritical women and to punish jealous fools like Pinchwife. Within the play, he arouses no disgust or contempt among the respectable characters. The most virtuous person, Alithea, regards him as a man of honor (V.iv.239) —that is, loyal to his friends, gentlemanly toward civil women, true to his word, and manly. Of other amiable qualities, we might note his sound judgment, his outstanding intelligence, his love of wit, his hatred of hypocrisy, his dislike of fools, and his contempt for incompetent husbands. Though formidable to loose women and stupid men, he is welcome among the wits. If he is more cynical than most wits, his cynicism seems vindicated by his experience. It should be noted too that Horner is, in some respects, victimized by his own intrigue and barely escapes being a comic figure himself. The plethora of mistresses proves an embarrassment of riches. His time is expropriated by a horde of women; he is reduced to those very activities he despises, of shopping for china and playing at cards with women; and at the end, he is very nearly trapped by the ardor that he has aroused in Margery. Thus we smile at Horner's involvement rather than feel shock at his success; his intrigue is indeed a comic one for all concerned.

As for his women "victims," Lady Fidget and her cohorts deserve their exposure. She is a mere pretender to honor, for she is as predatory as Horner and more unscrupulous than he. Her hypocritical concern for her "dear, dear honor" makes her a perfect object of satire. Mrs. Squeamish and Mrs. Dainty Fidget, as their names imply, show the same hypocritical concern for reputation and the same meretricious interest in sex; such "bigots" in honor, like "bigots" in religion, should be exposed, in the eyes of the audience if not of their own world. Mrs. Margery Pinchwife, though more honest than her counterparts among the women of quality, is a splendid female animal, amoral, clever, sensual, who follows her natural instincts and rushes willingly into the arms of Horner. Her mistakes, contrivances, and naiveté provide amusement and should not arouse any moral scruples in the audience.

The husbands likewise deserve no sympathy; for Sir Jasper Fidget and Pinchwife are no common cuckolds held up to ridicule because of their misfortune. Rather, the cuckolding is their due punishment— for stupidity, incompetence, lack of judgment, or absurd jealousy. Sir Jasper, the gullible fool who is all for business, while Horner takes care of his wife's business, is at once the simpleton, whose loud laughter betokens his empty mind, and the negligent husband who forgets his marital duties. Pinchwife, who could not hold on to his own whore in bachelor days, is that absurd husband who mistakenly believes he can have a wife to himself by keeping her ignorant and subservient, while at the same time denying her any wifely satisfactions, whether of the bed or the town. As the gullible or the absurdly jealous husband, Sir Jasper and Pinchwife share equally the satiric lashes of the author.

Central to their fates is Wycherley's notion of marriage, one of the main threads in *The Country Wife*. The two ridiculed husbands have the wrong attitude toward women and marriage. Sir Jasper, who neglects his wife, is cuckolded equally with Pinchwife, who tries to dominate his wife. Indifference or hostility constitute no basis for a happy relationship. Pinchwife, the more censurable of the two, regards women as natural enemies of men and believes a woman should be kept ignorant and docile so that the husband may have the upper hand. I understand the town, he says; but he does not understand women. His false assumptions lead to comic disaster for him. By denying Margery freedom, equality, and satisfaction, he only alienates her and encourages rebellion and loathing. Horner, though himself unsuited to marriage, is wiser when he says that women, like soldiers, are made constant by "good pay" (I.i. 434–435).

This theme of marriage has its clearest statement in the Harcourt-Alithea story, which contrasts with the other two stories. In this comic action, Alithea is at once the ideal heroine and the mistaken young woman, and she thus becomes a complex figure despite her few appearances. On the one hand, she is truly honorable, in contrast to Lady Fidget; having pledged herself to marry Sparkish, she remains true to her promise, despite ample demonstrations of his stupidity. She is also the typical young woman of Restoration comedy, fashionable, pleasure-loving, intelligent, with contempt for the country and appreciation for Harcourt's wit, though she may be wittier in her judgment than in either her action or words. On the other hand, she is the mistaken young woman who is at first persuaded by appearances that Sparkish is not jealous and that Harcourt is a loose gallant. The means of her "enlightenment" is Sparkish, who is at first as gullible as Sir Jasper and later as jealous as Pinchwife; his transformation reveals the truth to her. This comic episode of courtship brings together Harcourt and Alithea, two sophisticated people who, unlike Horner and Lady Fidget, are united by love rather than lust. Presumably their relationship, which will lead to marriage, will be free of absurd jealousy, infidelity, or the desire to dominate. The two are equally matched; and in a world of hypocritical and unfaithful wives, stupid and cruel husbands, jealous lovers, and rakes, these two move gracefully and securely. Their courtship, set off by the exposure and ridicule of Sparkish, is an episode free of cynicism and libertinism; and Harcourt addresses Alithea with mock seriousness, in the hyperbolical and idealized language of love, as "divine, heavenly creature" and "seraphic lady."

The counterpart of their courtship scene is the "china" scene, in which a different kind of lovers come together. Superficially, it is an immoral passage, with *double-entendre* and sexual wit. Yet it is an effective scene in which the comic possibilities are fully exploited in a witty manner. Sir Jasper is ridiculed for his credulity, Lady Fidget is exposed for a hypocritical libertine, and even Horner does not escape quite unscathed, being hard put to meet his commitments. Symbolically, too, as a supplier of "china" for all women, Horner exposes the limitations of the natural level on which he functions, in which there is no love and no permanency of relationship. Although an effective dramatic scene, in some ways superior to even the famous "screen" scene in Sheridan's *School for Scandal*, the "china" passage has occasioned more censure than any other episode in Restoration comedy. Wycherley apparently felt obliged to defend it, for *The Plain Dealer* has an exchange between the hypocritical Olivia and the common-sensical Eliza on this very scene. Olivia, who publicly loathes sex and yet is libertine, declares: "I say, the lewdest, filthiest thing is his china; nay, I will never forgive the beastly author his china; he has quite taken away the reputation of poor china itself, and sullied the most innocent and pretty furniture of a lady's chamber, insomuch that I was fain to break all of my defiled vessels." To Olivia's remark that *The Country Wife* is a filthy play, Eliza replies sensibly, "Faith, I dare swear the poor man did not think to disoblige the ladies by any amorous, soft, passionate, luscious saying in his play" (II.i).

The Country Wife, like *Lysistrata* or *Amphitryon* or any other comedy that turns on the subject of sex, is frank in its references. But it is never salacious in its dialogue or situations; the references are blunt rather than suggestive. In fact, the sexual episodes and allusions should rather disillusion than stimulate. Venereal disease, prostitutes, pimps, impotence, adultery, kept men—these are the images associated with sex. In contrast, we have the love of Harcourt and Alithea, completely free of sexual innuendos and overtures. Though her maid Lucy may be called a "strapper" by Dorilant and though she may have worldly views of a wife's freedom, Alithea herself remains a pure and honorable young woman whose chastity is a matter of concern to Harcourt.

But though the play is not licentious, its tone is libertine, cynical, and earthy. The characters who dominate the play are Horner, Margery, and Lady Fidget rather than Harcourt and Alithea. This is as it should be, for *The Country Wife* is a satirical comedy, in the tradition of classical satire. Though it lacks the *saeva indignatio* of Jonson's *Volpone*, for example, and though it does not war against such vices as avarice, lust, and gluttony, it exposes hypocrites, fools, and would-be wits. The object of satire is summed up in the words of Horner: "A pox on 'em, and all that force nature, and would be still what she forbids 'em! Affectation is her greatest monster" (I.i. 248–249). The "forcers" of nature—whether Pinchwife, who seeks to divert Margery from her instinctive search for pleasure, or Sir Jasper, who does not satisfy his wife's desires—for their violation of nature, are mercilessly satirized. Society is liberally peopled too with those guilty of affectation, whether it be in the ministry, in high society, or at court; among these, Wycherley singles out the pretenders to honor, for their hypocrisy and pretense. Also ridiculed is that affecter of wit, Sparkish, who would be a fashionable man, if he could. "Most men," as Harcourt says, "are the contraries to that they would seem" (I.i.250). Horner, in his intrigue, ironically assumes a guise too, and "affects" impotence so that he may expose real pretenders. And so the comedy of appearances goes its merry way.

Beyond this, the tone of *The Country Wife* depends on that vein of irony that runs through the entire play. Indeed, this is one of the most ironic plays in English. Situation after situation reveals its ironic complications, as the credulous Sir Jasper is cuckolded almost before his face or Pinchwife unwittingly thrusts his wife into Horner's arms. Horner is the supreme ironist, in his attitude and language; in his encounters with Pinchwife or Lady Fidget, he is at once complaisant and cynically detached. With Margery, he expends flattery in expectation of reward, though amused both by her ardor and her husband's stupidity. His words are double-edged, his mind split between commitment and detachment, his activities ambiguous in intent. As he moves through the play, the characters become embroiled in ironic situations, their remarks and actions at cross-purposes, while Horner looks on with amused detachment, like some spider watching the antics of trapped flies.

Something must be said too of Wycherley's style in establishing the tone of the play and the ironic undercurrent. Although it lacks the subtlety, balance, and beauty of Congreve's, the style of Wycherley is eminently suited to the stage and to his dramatic purpose. In its very bluntness and plainness, it drives home the comic point. A striking example is Horner's retort to the jealous Pinchwife:

PINCHWIFE.

I will not be a cuckold, I say; there will be danger in making me a cuckold.

HORNER.

Why, wert thou not well cured of thy last clap? (IV.iii. 299–301)

Wycherley's wit is less restrained and less subtle than Congreve's; but it strikes home no less effectively. His comic dialogue is often metaphoric in the characteristic manner of Restoration comedy; but the similitudes are homely, blunt, or realistic:

PINCHWIFE.

. . . A mask! No—a woman masked, like a covered dish, gives a man curiosity and appetite, when, it may be, uncovered, 'twould turn his stomach. (III.i.105–108)

On the stage, such direct dialogue effectively communicates its meaning. Within its limits of clarity, common sense, explicitness, even gross earthiness, this style of Wycherley's has considerable range. The characters are to some extent delineated by their speech. These marks of individuality are often mere idiosyncrasies of speech, like Margery's "indeed, and indeed," or Lady Fidget's "foh! foh!" or "my dear, dear honor." But the nonsense of Sparkish is pointed up by his verbosity and his rambling sentences: "I love to be envied, and would not marry a wife that I alone could love; loving alone is as dull as eating alone. Is it not a frank age? and I am a frank person. And to tell you the truth, it may be I love to have rivals in a wife, they make her seem to a man still but as a kept mistress; and so good night, for I must to Whitehall" (III.ii.348–353). There is also the charming humor and delicate irony of the exchange between Margery and Alithea:

MRS. PINCHWIFE.
He says he won't let me go abroad for fear of catching the pox.
ALITHEA.
Fie! the smallpox you should say. (II.i.30–32)

The forceful, vivid style of Wycherley's dramatic dialogue, with its supple and sinewy strength, its crude vigor and its earthiness, is eminently suited to the satire and irony of *The Country Wife*. This dialogue, at once colloquial and metaphorical and epigrammatic, gives unity of tone to the play; essentially, it is not realistic dialogue.

The Country Wife rises above realistic comedy into the realm of intellectual comedy. To be sure, the minute details of London life solidly anchor the play in the real world of Restoration England in the 1670's. There are numerous references to Whitehall, ordinaries, playhouses, venereal disease, drinking, card games, musical entertainments, masking, and loose women. But the play transcends this, and becomes pure comedy. The two-dimensional characterization and the almost farcical situations contribute to this effect. The dramatic action is simply, almost mechanically defined; the persons in the play are so many pawns manipulated by the author, their moves determined in part by the goal to be achieved. The roles are signified by the names: so the intriguer is Horner, the absurd husband is Pinchwife, the meretricious and stupid are Fidgets and Squeamishes. Contributing to the total effect are the wit and irony, providing in their own way a kind of esthetic distancing between audience and action. Though never rising to the brilliance of Molière's intellectual comedy, *The Country Wife* equally liberates us from the concretely realistic. Thus, while Wycherley's satire is caustic and his irony mordant, the final effect of the play is one of delight. We may be lightly stirred to indignation by the satirist, but we are more profoundly moved to intellectual laughter.

THOMAS H. FUJIMURA

University of Hawaii

Bibliography

EMMETT L. AVERY. "*The Country Wife* in the Eighteenth Century," *Research Studies of the State College of Washington*, X (1942), 142–158.

WILLARD CONNELY. *Brawny Wycherley*. London, 1930.

BONAMY DOBRÉE. *Restoration Comedy 1660–1720*. Oxford, 1924.

THOMAS H. FUJIMURA. *The Restoration Comedy of Wit*. Princeton, 1952.

HARLEY GRANVILLE-BARKER. "Wycherley and Dryden," *On Dramatic Method*. London, 1931.

NORMAN N. HOLLAND. *The First Modern Comedies*. Cambridge, Mass., 1959.

KATHLEEN M. LYNCH. *The Social Mode of Restoration Comedy*. New York, 1926.

ROBERT N. E. MEGAW. "The Two 1695 Editions of Wycherley's *Country-Wife*," *Studies in Bibliography*, III (1950–1951), 252–253.

JOHN PALMER. *The Comedy of Manners*. London, 1913.

CHARLES PERROMAT. *William Wycherley, Sa Vie, Son Oeuvre*. Paris, 1921.

HENRY TEN EYCK PERRY. *The Comic Spirit in Restoration Drama*. New Haven, 1925.

JOHN HARRINGTON SMITH. *The Gay Couple in Restoration Comedy*. Cambridge, Mass., 1948.

HOWARD P. VINCENT. "The Death of William Wycherley," *Harvard Studies and Notes in Philology and Literature*, XV (1933), 219–242.

JOHN WILCOX. *The Relation of Molière to Restoration Comedy*. New York, 1938.

JOHN HAROLD WILSON. *The Court Wits of the Restoration*. Princeton, 1948.

THE COUNTRY WIFE

Indignor quicquam reprehendi, non quia crasse
Compositum illepideve putetur, sed quia nuper:
Nec veniam antiquis, sed honorem et praemia posci.

Horat.

I hate to see something criticized, not because it is
clumsy and inelegant, but because it is modern; and
not only indulgence but honors and rewards demanded
for the old writers. —Horace *Epistles* II. 1. 76–78.

Prologue
Spoken by Mr. Hart

Poets, like cudgel'd bullies, never do
At first or second blow submit to you;
But will provoke you still, and ne'er have done,
Till you are weary first with laying on.
The late so baffled scribbler of this day,   5
Though he stands trembling, bids me boldly say,
What we before most plays are us'd to do,
For poets out of fear first draw on you;
In a fierce prologue the still pit defy,
And ere you speak, like Castril give the lie.   10
But though our Bayes's battles oft I've fought,
And with bruis'd knuckles their dear conquests bought;
Nay, never yet fear'd odds upon the stage,
In prologue dare not hector with the age,
But would take quarter from your saving hands,   15
Though Bayes within all yielding countermands,
Says you confed'rate wits no quarter give,
Therefore his play shan't ask your leave to live.
Well, let the vain rash fop, by huffing so,
Think to obtain the better terms of you;   20
But we, the actors, humbly will submit,
Now, and at any time, to a full pit;
Nay, often we anticipate your rage,
And murder poets for you on our stage.
We set no guards upon our tiring-room,   25
But when with flying colors there you come,
We patiently, you see, give up to you
Our poets, virgins, nay, our matrons too.

---

1. *bullies*] common nuisances in London, characterized by hectoring and huffing.

5. *baffled scribbler*] possible reference to ill success of *The Gentleman Dancing-Master* (1672).

10. *Castril*] the "angry boy" in Jonson's *Alchemist* (1610).

11. *Bayes's*] poet's.

The Persons

MR. HORNER	*Mr. Hart*
MR. HARCOURT	*Mr. Kynaston*
MR. DORILANT	*Mr. Lydal*
MR. PINCHWIFE	*Mr. Mohun*
MR. SPARKISH	*Mr. Haines*
SIR JASPER FIDGET	*Mr. Cartwright*
MRS. MARGERY PINCHWIFE	*Mrs. Boutell*
MRS. ALITHEA	*Mrs. James*
MY LADY FIDGET	*Mrs. Knep*
MRS. DAINTY FIDGET	*Mrs. Corbet*
MRS. SQUEAMISH	*Mrs. Wyatt*
OLD LADY SQUEAMISH	*Mrs. Rutter*

WAITERS, SERVANTS, AND ATTENDANTS
A BOY

A QUACK	*Mr. Shatterel*
LUCY, ALITHEA'S MAID	*Mrs. Cory*

The Scene: *London*

The Country Wife

[I.i] *Enter* Horner, *and* Quack *following him at a distance.*

HORNER (*aside*).

A quack is as fit for a pimp as a midwife for a bawd; they
are still but in their way both helpers of nature. —Well, my
dear doctor, hast thou done what I desired?

QUACK.

I have undone you forever with the women, and reported
you throughout the whole town as bad as a eunuch, with   5
as much trouble as if I had made you one in earnest.

HORNER.

But have you told all the midwives you know, the orange-
wenches at the playhouses, the city husbands, and old
fumbling keepers of this end of the town? for they'll be the
readiest to report it.   10

QUACK.

I have told all the chambermaids, waiting-women, tire-
women, and old women of my acquaintance; nay, and
whispered it as a secret to 'em, and to the whisperers of
Whitehall; so that you need not doubt 'twill spread, and
you will be as odious to the handsome young women as—   15

HORNER.

As the smallpox. Well—

QUACK.

And to the married women of this end of the town as—

HORNER.

As the great ones; nay, as their own husbands.

QUACK.

And to the city dames as aniseed Robin of filthy and
contemptible memory; and they will frighten their children   20

---

11. all] *Q1–2, 4–5, O; om. Q3.*

---

19. *aniseed Robin*] Robin Goodfellow, a prankish sprite.

–5–

with your name, especially their females.

HORNER.

And cry, "Horner's coming to carry you away." I am only
afraid 'twill not be believed. You told 'em 'twas by an
English-French disaster, and an English-French surgeon,
who has given me at once not only a cure but an antidote　25
for the future against that damned malady, and that
worse distemper, love, and all other women's evils?

QUACK.

Your late journey into France has made it the more credible,
and your being here a fortnight before you appeared in
public looks as if you apprehended the shame, which I　30
wonder you do not. Well, I have been hired by young
gallants to belie 'em t'other way; but you are the first
would be thought a man unfit for women.

HORNER.

Dear Mr. Doctor, let vain rogues be contented only to be
thought abler men than they are, generally 'tis all the　35
pleasure they have; but mine lies another way.

QUACK.

You take, methinks, a very preposterous way to it, and as
ridiculous as if we operators in physic should put forth bills
to disparage our medicaments, with hopes to gain customers.

HORNER.

Doctor, there are quacks in love as well as physic, who get　40
but the fewer and worse patients for their boasting; a good
name is seldom got by giving it oneself, and women no more
than honor are compassed by bragging. Come, come, doctor,
the wisest lawyer never discovers the merits of his cause till
the trial; the wealthiest man conceals his riches, and the　45
cunning gamester his play. Shy husbands and keepers, like
old rooks, are not to be cheated but by a new unpracticed
trick; false friendship will pass now no more than false dice
upon 'em; no, not in the city.

48. pass] *Q 1–5; om. O.*

---

24. *English-French disaster*] venereal disease (French pox) caught from an
English whore.
44. *discovers*] reveals.
47. *rooks*] sharpers, cheats.

Enter Boy.

BOY.

There are two ladies and a gentleman coming up.   [*Exit.*] 50

HORNER.

A pox! some unbelieving sisters of my former acquaintance, who, I am afraid, expect their sense should be satisfied of the falsity of the report. No—this formal fool and women!

Enter Sir Jasper Fidget, Lady Fidget, *and* Mrs. Dainty Fidget.

QUACK.

His wife and sister.

SIR JASPER FIDGET.

My coach breaking just now before your door, sir, I look   55
upon as an occasional reprimand to me, sir, for not kissing your hands, sir, since your coming out of France, sir; and so my disaster, sir, has been my good fortune, sir; and this is my wife and sister, sir.

HORNER.

What then, sir?   60

SIR JASPER FIDGET.

My lady, and sister, sir. —Wife, this is Master Horner.

LADY FIDGET.

Master Horner, husband!

SIR JASPER FIDGET.

My lady, my Lady Fidget, sir.

HORNER.

So, sir.

SIR JASPER FIDGET.

Won't you be acquainted with her sir? —(*Aside.*) So, the   65
report is true, I find, by his coldness or aversion to the sex; but I'll play the wag with him. —Pray salute my wife, my lady, sir.

HORNER.

I will kiss no man's wife, sir, for him, sir; I have taken my eternal leave, sir, of the sex already, sir.   70

---

51. *pox*] venereal disease, sometimes called the French pox.
56. *occasional*] timely.

SIR JASPER FIDGET (*aside*).

Ha, ha, ha! I'll plague him yet. —Not know my wife, sir?

HORNER.

I do know your wife, sir; she's a woman, sir, and consequently a monster, sir, a greater monster than a husband, sir.

SIR JASPER FIDGET.

A husband! how, sir?

HORNER.

So, sir; but I make no more cuckolds, sir.   75

(*Makes horns.*)

SIR JASPER FIDGET.

Ha, ha, ha! Mercury, Mercury!

LADY FIDGET.

Pray, Sir Jasper', let us be gone from this rude fellow.

MRS. DAINTY FIDGET.

Who, by his breeding, would think he had ever been in
France?

LADY FIDGET.

Foh! he's but too much a French fellow, such as hate women   80
of quality and virtue for their love to their husbands, Sir
Jasper; a woman is hated by 'em as much for loving her
husband as for loving their money. But pray let's be gone.

HORNER.

You do well, madam, for I have nothing that you came for.
I have brought over not so much as a bawdy picture, new   85
postures, nor the second part of the *École des Filles*, nor—

QUACK (*apart to* Horner).

Hold, for shame, sir! What d'ye mean? You'll ruin yourself
forever with the sex—

SIR JASPER FIDGET.

Ha, ha, ha! He hates women perfectly, I find.

MRS. DAINTY FIDGET.

What pity 'tis he should.   90

LADY FIDGET.

Ay, he's a base, rude fellow for't; but affectation makes not

---

75.1. *Makes horns*] mark of the cuckold.
76. *Mercury*] used in treatment of venereal disease.
85–86. *new postures*] indecent engravings printed with Aretino's lewd poems.
86. *École des Filles*] a pornographic book.

a woman more odious to them than virtue.

HORNER.

Because your virtue is your greatest affectation, madam.

LADY FIDGET.

How, you saucy fellow! Would you wrong my honor?

HORNER.

If I could.   95

LADY FIDGET.

How d'ye mean, sir?

SIR JASPER FIDGET.

Ha, ha, ha! No, he can't wrong your ladyship's honor, upon
my honor; he, poor man—hark you in your ear—a mere
eunuch.

LADY FIDGET.

O filthy French beast! foh, foh! Why do we stay? Let's be 100
gone; I can't endure the sight of him.

SIR JASPER FIDGET.

Stay but till the chairs come; they'll be here presently.

LADY FIDGET.

No, no.

SIR JASPER FIDGET.

Nor can I stay longer. 'Tis—let me see, a quarter and a half
quarter of a minute past eleven; the council will be sat, I 105
must away. Business must be preferred always before love
and ceremony with the wise, Mr. Horner.

HORNER.

And the impotent, Sir Jasper.

SIR JASPER FIDGET.

Ay, ay, the impotent, Master Horner, ha, ha, ha!

LADY FIDGET.

What, leave us with a filthy man alone in his lodgings?   110

SIR JASPER FIDGET.

He's an innocent man now, you know. Pray stay, I'll
hasten the chairs to you. —Mr. Horner, your servant; I
should be glad to see you at my house. Pray come and dine
with me, and play at cards with my wife after dinner; you
are fit for women at that game yet, ha, ha! —(*Aside.*) 'Tis 115

---

102. *chairs*] sedan chairs.

as much a husband's prudence to provide innocent diversion for a wife as to hinder her unlawful pleasures, and he had better employ her than let her employ herself. —Farewell.

HORNER.

Your servant, Sir Jasper.   *Exit* Sir Jasper.

LADY FIDGET.

I will not stay with him, foh!   120

HORNER.

Nay, madam, I beseech you stay, if it be but to see I can be as civil to ladies yet as they would desire.

LADY FIDGET.

No, no, fòh! You cannot be civil to ladies.

MRS. DAINTY FIDGET.

You as civil as ladies would desire?

LADY FIDGET.

No, no, no! foh, foh, foh!   125

Exeunt Lady Fidget *and* [Mrs.] Dainty.

QUACK.

Now, I think, I, or you yourself rather, have done your business with the women.

HORNER.

Thou art an ass. Don't you see already, upon the report and my carriage, this grave man of business leaves his wife in my lodgings, invites me to his house and wife, who before would 130 not be acquainted with me out of jealousy?

QUACK.

Nay, by this means you may be the more acquainted with the husbands, but the less with the wives.

HORNER.

Let me alone; if I can but abuse the husbands, I'll soon disabuse the wives. Stay—I'll reckon you up the advantages 135 I am like to have by my stratagem: First, I shall be rid of all my old acquaintances, the most insatiable sorts of duns, that invade our lodgings in a morning. And next to the pleasure of making a new mistress is that of being rid of an old one, and of all old debts; love, when it comes to be so, is 140 paid the most unwillingly.

137. sorts] *Q1–4, O;* sort *Q5.*

QUACK.

Well, you may be so rid of your old acquaintances; but how will you get any new ones?

HORNER.

Doctor, thou wilt never make a good chemist, thou art so incredulous and impatient. Ask but all the young fellows of 145 the town if they do not lose more time, like huntsmen, in starting the game than in running it down; one knows not where to find 'em, who will or will not. Women of quality are so civil you can hardly distinguish love from good breeding, and a man is often mistaken; but now I can be 150 sure she that shows an aversion to me loves the sport, as those women that are gone, whom I warrant to be right. And then the next thing is, your women of honor, as you call 'em, are only chary of their reputations, not their persons, and 'tis scandal they would avoid, not men. Now may I have, 155 by the reputation of a eunuch, the privileges of one; and be seen in a lady's chamber in a morning as early as her husband; kiss virgins before their parents or lovers; and may be, in short, the *passe partout* of the town. Now, doctor.

QUACK.

Nay, now you shall be the doctor; and your process is so new 160 that we do not know but it may succeed.

HORNER.

Not so new neither; *probatum est,* doctor.

QUACK.

Well, I wish you luck and many patients whilst I go to mine.

Exit Quack.

Enter Harcourt *and* Dorilant *to* Horner.

HARCOURT.

Come, your appearance at the play yesterday has, I hope, hardened you for the future against the women's contempt 165 and the men's raillery; and now you'll abroad as you were wont.

---

144. *chemist*] alchemist looking for philosopher's stone.
152. *right*] cant for loose women.
162. *probatum est*] it has been proved, tested.

HORNER.

Did I not bear it bravely?

DORILANT.

With a most theatrical impudence; nay, more than the
orange-wenches show there, or a drunken vizard-mask, or a   170
great-bellied actress; nay, or the most impudent of creatures,
an ill poet; or what is yet more impudent, a secondhand
critic.

HORNER.

But what say the ladies? Have they no pity?

HARCOURT.

What ladies? The vizard-masks, you know, never pity a   175
man when all's gone, though in their service.

DORILANT.

And for the women in the boxes, you'd never pity them
when 'twas in your power.

HARCOURT.

They say, 'tis pity but all that deal with common women
should be served so.   180

DORILANT.

Nay, I dare swear, they won't admit you to play at cards
with them, go to plays with 'em, or do the little duties
which other shadows of men are wont to do for 'em.

HORNER.

Who do you call shadows of men?

DORILANT.

Half-men.   185

HORNER.

What, boys?

DORILANT.

Ay, your old boys, old *beaux garçons*, who, like superannuated
stallions, are suffered to run, feed, and whinny with the mares
as long as they live, though they can do nothing else.

177. women] *Q 1–4, O;* woman *Q 5.*

---

170. *vizard-mask*] whore.
187. *old beaux garçons*] worn-out rakes.

HORNER.

Well, a pox on love and wenching! Women serve but to 190
keep a man from better company; though I can't enjoy
them, I shall you the more. Good fellowship and friendship
are lasting, rational, and manly pleasures.

HARCOURT.

For all that, give me some of those pleasures you call
effeminate too; they help to relish one another.   195

HORNER.

They disturb one another.

HARCOURT.

No, mistresses are like books. If you pore upon them too
much, they doze you and make you unfit for company; but
if used discreetly, you are the fitter for conversation by 'em.

DORILANT.

A mistress should be like a little country retreat near the 200
town, not to dwell in constantly, but only for a night and
away, to taste the town the better when a man returns.

HORNER.

I tell you, 'tis as hard to be a good fellow, a good friend, and
a lover of women, as 'tis to be a good fellow, a good
friend, and a lover of money. You cannot follow both, then 205
choose your side. Wine gives you liberty, love takes it away.

DORILANT.

Gad, he's in the right on't.

HORNER.

Wine gives you joy; love, grief and tortures, besides the
surgeon's. Wine makes us witty; love, only sots. Wine
makes us sleep; love breaks it.   210

DORILANT.

By the world, he has reason, Harcourt.

HORNER.

Wine makes—

DORILANT.

Ay, wine makes us—makes us princes; love makes us beggars,

212. makes] *Q 1-2, 4-5, O;* makes   213. wine makes us] *Q 1-4, O;*
us *Q 3.*   wine makes *Q 5.*

198. *doze*] muddle, confuse.

poor rogues, egad—and wine—

HORNER.

So, there's one converted. —No, no, love and wine, oil and 215
vinegar.

HARCOURT.

I grant it; love will still be uppermost.

HORNER.

Come, for my part I will have only those glorious, manly
pleasures of being very drunk and very slovenly.

Enter Boy.

BOY.

Mr. Sparkish is below, sir.   [*Exit.*] 220

HARCOURT.

What, my dear friend! a rogue that is fond of me only, I
think, for abusing him.

DORILANT.

No, he can no more think the men laugh at him than that
women jilt him, his opinion of himself is so good.

HORNER.

Well, there's another pleasure by drinking I thought not of; 225
I shall lose his acquaintance, because he cannot drink; and
you know 'tis a very hard thing to be rid of him, for he's one
of those nauseous offerers at wit, who, like the worst fiddlers,
run themselves into all companies.

HARCOURT.

One that, by being in the company of men of sense, would 230
pass for one.

HORNER.

And may so to the shortsighted world, as a false jewel
amongst true ones is not discerned at a distance. His
company is as troublesome to us as a cuckold's when you
have a mind to his wife's.   235

HARCOURT.

No, the rogue will not let us enjoy one another, but ravishes
our conversation, though he signifies no more to't than

232. to] *Q 1–4, O; om. Q 5.*

---

228. *offerers*] attempters.

Sir Martin Mar-all's gaping, and awkward thrumming
upon the lute, does to his man's voice and music.

DORILANT.

And to pass for a wit in town shows himself a fool every 240
night to us, that are guilty of the plot.

HORNER.

Such wits as he are, to a company of reasonable men, like
rooks to the gamesters, who only fill a room at the table,
but are so far from contributing to the play that they only
serve to spoil the fancy of those that do.   245

DORILANT.

Nay, they are used like rooks too, snubbed, checked, and
abused; yet the rogues will hang on.

HORNER.

A pox on 'em, and all that force nature, and would be still
what she forbids 'em! Affectation is her greatest monster.

HARCOURT.

Most men are the contraries to that they would seem. Your 250
bully, you see, is a coward with a long sword; the little,
humbly fawning physician, with his ebony cane, is he that
destroys men.

DORILANT.

The usurer, a poor rogue possessed of moldy bonds and
mortgages; and we they call spendthrifts are only wealthy, 255
who lay out his money upon daily new purchases of pleasure.

HORNER.

Ay, your arrantest cheat is your trustee, or executor; your
jealous man, the greatest cuckold; your churchman, the
greatest atheist; and your noisy, pert rogue of a wit, the
greatest fop, dullest ass, and worst company, as you shall see. 260
For here he comes.

Enter Sparkish *to them.*

SPARKISH.

How is't, sparks, how is't? Well, faith, Harry, I must rally

---

238. *Sir Martin Mar-all*] fool in Dryden's comedy of that name (1667)
who pretends to serenade his mistress with a lute while his concealed
servant sings.

thee a little, ha, ha, ha! upon the report in town of thee,
ha, ha, ha! I can't hold i' faith; shall I speak?

HORNER.

Yes, but you'll be so bitter then.   265

SPARKISH.

Honest Dick and Frank here shall answer for me, I will not
be extreme bitter, by the universe.

HARCOURT.

We will be bound in ten thousand pound bond, he shall
not be bitter at all.

DORILANT.

Nor sharp, nor sweet.   270

HORNER.

What, not downright insipid?

SPARKISH.

Nay then, since you are so brisk and provoke me, take what
follows. You must know, I was discoursing and rallying with
some ladies yesterday, and they happened to talk of the fine
new signs in town.   275

HORNER.

Very fine ladies, I believe.

SPARKISH.

Said I, "I know where the best new sign is." "Where?"
says one of the ladies. "In Covent Garden," I replied. Said
another, "In what street?" "In Russell Street," answered I.
"Lord," says another, "I'm sure there was ne'er a fine new   280
sign there yesterday." "Yes, but there was," said I again,
"and it came out of France, and has been there a fortnight."

DORILANT.

A pox! I can hear no more, prithee.

HORNER.

No, hear him out; let him tune his crowd a while.

HARCOURT.

The worst music, the greatest preparation.   285

---

278. *Covent Garden*] district in fashionable West End London.
279. *Russell Street*] fashionable residential area.
284. *crowd*] fiddle.

SPARKISH.

Nay, faith, I'll make you laugh. "It cannot be," says a third lady. "Yes, yes," quoth I again. Says a fourth lady—

HORNER.

Look to't, we'll have no more ladies.

SPARKISH.

No—then mark, mark, now. Said I to the fourth, "Did you never see Mr. Horner? He lodges in Russell Street, and he's 290 a sign of a man, you know, since he came out of France." He, ha, he!

HORNER.

But the devil take me, if thine be the sign of a jest.

SPARKISH.

With that they all fell a-laughing, till they bepissed themselves! What, but it does not move you, methinks? Well, I 295 see one had as good go to law without a witness, as break a jest without a laugher on one's side. Come, come, sparks, but where do we dine? I have left at Whitehall an earl to dine with you.

DORILANT.

Why, I thought thou hadst loved a man with a title better 300 than a suit with a French trimming to't.

HARCOURT.

Go to him again.

SPARKISH.

No, sir, a wit to me is the greatest title in the world.

HORNER.

But go dine with your earl, sir; he may be exceptious. We are your friends, and will not take it ill to be left, I do assure 305 you.

HARCOURT.

Nay, faith, he shall go to him.

SPARKISH.

Nay, pray, gentlemen.

DORILANT.

We'll thrust you out, if you wo'not. What, disappoint

295. I] *Q 3, O; om. Q 1–2, 4–5.*   297. laugher] *Q 1;* laughter *Q 2–5,*
                                            O.

anybody for us?   310

SPARKISH.

Nay, dear gentlemen, hear me.

HORNER.

No, no, sir, by no means; pray go, sir.

SPARKISH.

Why, dear rogues—

DORILANT.

No, no.   (*They all thrust him out of the room.*)

ALL.

Ha, ha, ha!   315

Sparkish *returns.*

SPARKISH.

But, sparks, pray hear me. What, d'ye think I'll eat then with
gay, shallow fops and silent coxcombs? I think wit as
necessary at dinner as a glass of good wine, and that's the
reason I never have any stomach when I eat alone.
—Come, but where do we dine?   320

HORNER.

Even where you will.

SPARKISH.

At Chateline's?

DORILANT.

Yes, if you will.

SPARKISH.

Or at the Cock?

DORILANT.

Yes, if you please.   325

SPARKISH.

Or at the Dog and Partridge?

HORNER.

Ay, if you have a mind to't, for we shall dine at neither.

SPARKISH.

Pshaw! with your fooling we shall lose the new play; and I

327. a mind] *Q 2–5, O;* mind *Q 1.*

---

322. *Chateline's*] fashionable French ordinary (restaurant) in Covent
Garden.
324. *Cock*] tavern in Bow Street.
326. *Dog and Partridge*] tavern in Fleet Street.

would no more miss seeing a new play the first day than I
would miss sitting in the wits' row. Therefore I'll go fetch 330
my mistress and away.   *Exit* Sparkish.

Manent Horner, Harcourt, Dorilant. *Enter to them* Mr. Pinchwife.

HORNER.

Who have we here? Pinchwife?

PINCHWIFE.

Gentlemen, your humble servant.

HORNER.

Well, Jack, by thy long absence from the town, the grumness
of thy countenance, and the slovenliness of thy habit, I 335
should give thee joy, should I not, of marriage?

PINCHWIFE (*aside*).

Death! does he know I'm married too? I thought to have
concealed it from him at least. —My long stay in the
country will excuse my dress, and I have a suit of law, that
brings me up to town, that puts me out of humor; besides, 340
I must give Sparkish tomorrow five thousand pound to lie
with my sister.

HORNER.

Nay, you country gentlemen, rather than not purchase,
will buy anything; and he is a cracked title, if we may
quibble. Well, but am I to give thee joy? I heard thou 345
wert married.

PINCHWIFE.

What then?

HORNER.

Why, the next thing that is to be heard is, thou'rt a cuckold.

PINCHWIFE (*aside*).

Insupportable name!

HORNER.

But I did not expect marriage from such a whoremaster as 350
you, one that knew the town so much, and women so well.

PINCHWIFE.

Why, I have married no London wife.

330. sitting] *Q 3;* setting *Q 1–2, 4–5,*
O.

---

334. *grumness*] moroseness.

HORNER.

Pshaw! that's all one; that grave circumspection in marrying
a country wife is like refusing a deceitful, pampered
Smithfield jade to go and be cheated by a friend in the 355
country.

PINCHWIFE (*aside*).

A pox on him and his simile! —At least we are a little
surer of the breed there, know what her keeping has been,
whether foiled or unsound.

HORNER.

Come, come, I have known a clap gotten in Wales; and 360
there are cousins, justices' clerks, and chaplains in the
country, I won't say coachmen. But she's handsome and
young?

PINCHWIFE (*aside*).

I'll answer as I should do. —No, no, she has no beauty but
her youth; no attraction but her modesty; wholesome, 365
homely, and housewifely; that's all.

DORILANT.

He talks as like a grazier as he looks.

PINCHWIFE.

She's too awkward, ill-favored, and silly to bring to town.

HARCOURT.

Then methinks you should bring her, to be taught breeding.

PINCHWIFE.

To be taught! no, sir, I thank you. Good wives and private 370
soldiers should be ignorant. —[*Aside.*] I'll keep her from
your instructions, I warrant you.

HARCOURT (*aside*).

The rogue is as jealous as if his wife were not ignorant.

HORNER.

Why, if she be ill-favored, there will be less danger here for
you than by leaving her in the country; we have such 375

357. a little] *Q1;* little *Q2–5, O.*

---

355. *Smithfield jade*] worn-out horse "freshened up" for sale to the
gullible at Smithfield; also disreputable woman.
359. *foiled*] injured, defective.
367. *grazier*] grazer of cattle.

variety of dainties that we are seldom hungry.

DORILANT.

But they have always coarse, constant, swingeing stomachs
in the country.

HARCOURT.

Foul feeders indeed.

DORILANT.

And your hospitality is great there.   380

HARCOURT.

Open house, every man's welcome.

PINCHWIFE.

So, so, gentlemen.

HORNER.

But, prithee, why wouldst thou marry her? If she be ugly,
ill-bred, and silly, she must be rich then.

PINCHWIFE.

As rich as if she brought me twenty thousand pound out of 385
this town; for she'll be as sure not to spend her moderate
portion as a London baggage would be to spend hers, let it
be what it would; so 'tis all one. Then, because she's ugly,
she's the likelier to be my own; and being ill-bred, she'll
hate conversation; and since silly and innocent, will not 390
know the difference betwixt a man of one-and-twenty and
one of forty.

HORNER.

Nine—to my knowledge; but if she be silly, she'll expect
as much from a man of forty-nine as from him of one-and-
twenty.   But methinks wit is more necessary than beauty, 395
and I think no young woman ugly that has it, and no
handsome woman agreeable without it.

PINCHWIFE.

'Tis my maxim, he's a fool that marries, but he's a greater
that does not marry a fool. What is wit in a wife good for,
but to make a man a cuckold?   400

HORNER.

Yes, to keep it from his knowledge.

---

377. *swingeing stomachs*] large appetites.
384. *silly*] ignorant.

PINCHWIFE.

A fool cannot contrive to make her husband a cuckold.

HORNER.

No, but she'll club with a man that can; and what is worse, if she cannot make her husband a cuckold, she'll make him jealous, and pass for one, and then 'tis all one. 405

PINCHWIFE.

Well, well, I'll take care for one, my wife shall make me no cuckold, though she had your help, Mr. Horner; I understand the town, sir.

DORILANT (*aside*).

His help!

HARCOURT (*aside*).

He's come newly to town, it seems, and has not heard how 410 things are with him.

HORNER.

But tell me, has marriage cured thee of whoring, which it seldom does?

HARCOURT.

'Tis more than age can do.

HORNER.

No, the word is, I'll marry and live honest; but a marriage 415 vow is like a penitent gamester's oath, and entering into bonds and penalties to stint himself to such a particular small sum at play for the future, which makes him but the more eager, and not being able to hold out, loses his money again, and his forfeit to boot. 420

DORILANT.

Ay, ay, a gamester will be a gamester whilst his money lasts, and a whoremaster whilst his vigor.

HARCOURT.

Nay, I have known 'em, when they are broke and can lose no more, keep a-fumbling with the box in their hands to fool with only, and hinder other gamesters. 425

DORILANT.

That had wherewithal to make lusty stakes.

---

415. *honest*] chaste.
416–417. *entering . . . penalties*] binding himself to penalties.
424. *box*] dice box.

PINCHWIFE.

Well, gentlemen, you may laugh at me, but you shall never
lie with my wife; I know the town.

HORNER.

But prithee, was not the way you were in better? Is not
keeping better than marriage?   430

PINCHWIFE.

A pox on't! The jades would jilt me; I could never keep a
whore to myself.

HORNER.

So, then you only married to keep a whore to yourself.
Well, but let me tell you, women, as you say, are like
soldiers, made constant and loyal by good pay rather than 435
by oaths and covenants. Therefore I'd advise my friends to
keep rather than marry, since too I find, by your example,
it does not serve one's turn; for I saw you yesterday in the
eighteen-penny place with a pretty country wench.

PINCHWIFE (*aside*).

How the devil! Did he see my wife then? I sat there that she 440
might not be seen. But she shall never go to a play again.

HORNER.

What, dost thou blush at nine-and-forty, for having been
seen with a wench?

DORILANT.

No, faith, I warrant 'twas his wife, which he seated there out
of sight, for he's a cunning rogue and understands the town. 445

HARCOURT.

He blushes. Then 'twas his wife, for men are now more
ashamed to be seen with them in public than with a wench.

PINCHWIFE (*aside*).

Hell and damnation! I'm undone, since Horner has seen
her, and they know 'twas she.

HORNER.

But prithee, was it thy wife? She was exceedingly pretty; I 450
was in love with her at that distance.

PINCHWIFE.

You are like never to be nearer to her. Your servant,

448. (*aside*)] *Q 1–2, 4–5, O; om. Q 3.*

---

439. *eighteen-penny place*] middle gallery in theatre, frequented by whores.

gentlemen. (*Offers to go.*)

PINCHWIFE.

Nay, prithee stay.

PINCHWIFE.

I cannot, I will not. 455

HORNER.

Come, you shall dine with us.

PINCHWIFE.

I have dined already.

HORNER.

Come, I know thou hast not. I'll treat thee, dear rogue;
thou shalt spend none of thy Hampshire money today.

PINCHWIFE (*aside*).

Treat me! So, he uses me already like his cuckold. 460

HORNER.

Nay, you shall not go.

PINCHWIFE.

I must, I have business at home. *Exit* Pinchwife.

HARCOURT.

To beat his wife; he's as jealous of her as a Cheapside
husband of a Covent Garden wife.

HORNER.

Why, 'tis as hard to find an old whoremaster without 465
jealousy and the gout, as a young one without fear or the
pox.
As gout in age from pox in youth proceeds,
So wenching past, then jealousy succeeds,
The worst disease that love and wenching breeds. 470

[*Exeunt.*]

[II.i] Mrs. Margery Pinchwife *and* Alithea.
Mr. Pinchwife *peeping behind at the door.*

MRS. PINCHWIFE.

Pray, sister, where are the best fields and woods to walk in,
in London?

---

453. *Offers*] attempts.
459. *Hampshire*] common term for the country.
463–464. *Cheapside husband*] city husband.
464. *Covent Garden wife*] fashionable wife, not of citizen class.

ALITHEA.

A pretty question! Why, sister, Mulberry Garden and St. James's Park; and for close walks, the New Exchange.

MRS. PINCHWIFE.

Pray, sister, tell me why my husband looks so grum here in   5
town, and keeps me up so close, and will not let me go a-walking, nor let me wear my best gown yesterday.

ALITHEA.

Oh, he's jealous, sister.

MRS. PINCHWIFE.

Jealous? What's that?

ALITHEA.

He's afraid you should love another man.   10

MRS. PINCHWIFE.

How should he be afraid of my loving another man, when he will not let me see any but himself?

ALITHEA.

Did he not carry you yesterday to a play?

MRS. PINCHWIFE.

Ay, but we sat amongst ugly people; he would not let me come near the gentry, who sat under us, so that I could not   15
see 'em. He told me none but naughty women sat there, whom they toused and moused. But I would have ventured for all that.

ALITHEA.

But how did you like the play?

MRS. PINCHWIFE.

Indeed, I was a-weary of the play, but I liked hugeously the   20
actors; they are the goodliest, properest men, sister!

ALITHEA.

Oh, but you must not like the actors, sister.

MRS. PINCHWIFE.

Ay, how should I help it, sister? Pray, sister, when my

20. a-weary] *Q1;* weary *Q2–5, O.*

---

3. *Mulberry Garden*] fashionable walk.
3–4. *St. James's Park*] noted for its Mall.
4. *New Exchange*] building with fashionable shops, in the Strand.
5. *grum*] morose.
17. *toused and moused*] rumpled and toyed with.

husband comes in, will you ask leave for me to go a-walking?

ALITHEA (*aside*).

A-walking! Ha, ha! Lord, a country gentlewoman's leisure 25
is the drudgery of a foot-post; and she requires as much
airing as her husband's horses.

Enter Mr. Pinchwife *to them.*

But here comes your husband; I'll ask, though I'm sure he'll
not grant it.

MRS. PINCHWIFE.

He says he won't let me go abroad for fear of catching the 30
pox.

ALITHEA.

Fie! the smallpox you should say.

MRS. PINCHWIFE.

O my dear, dear bud, welcome home! Why dost thou look
so fropish? Who has nangered thee?

PINCHWIFE.

You're a fool. 35

(Mrs. Pinchwife *goes aside and cries.*)

ALITHEA.

Faith, so she is, for crying for no fault, poor tender creature!

PINCHWIFE.

What, you would have her as impudent as yourself, as
arrant a jill-flirt, a gadder, a magpie, and to say all, a mere,
notorious town-woman?

ALITHEA.

Brother, you are my only censurer; and the honor of your 40
family shall sooner suffer in your wife there than in me,
though I take the innocent liberty of the town.

PINCHWIFE.

Hark you, mistress, do not talk so before my wife. The
innocent liberty of the town!

ALITHEA.

Why, pray, who boasts of any intrigue with me? What 45
lampoon has made my name notorious? What ill women

25. leisure] *Q1;* pleasure *Q2–5, O.*

---

34. *fropish*] peevish.   34. *nangered*] angered.
38. *jill-flirt*] wanton or giddy young woman.

frequent my lodgings? I keep no company with any women
of scandalous reputations.

PINCHWIFE.

No, you keep the men of scandalous reputations company.

ALITHEA.

Where? Would you not have me civil? answer 'em in a box   50
at the plays, in the drawing room at Whitehall, in St. James's
Park, Mulberry Garden, or—

PINCHWIFE.

Hold, hold! Do not teach my wife where the men are to be
found! I believe she's the worse for your town documents
already. I bid you keep her in ignorance, as I do.   55

MRS. PINCHWIFE.

Indeed, be not angry with her, bud; she will tell me nothing
of the town, though I ask her a thousand times a day.

PINCHWIFE.

Then you are very inquisitive to know, I find!

MRS. PINCHWIFE.

Not I, indeed, dear; I hate London. Our place-house in the
country is worth a thousand of't; would I were there again!   60

PINCHWIFE.

So you shall, I warrant. But were you not talking of plays
and players when I came in? —[To Alithea.]   You are
her encourager in such discourses.

MRS. PINCHWIFE.

No, indeed, dear; she chid me just now for liking the
playermen.   65

PINCHWIFE (aside).

Nay, if she be so innocent as to own to me her liking them,
there is no hurt in't. —Come, my poor rogue, but thou
lik'st none better than me?

MRS. PINCHWIFE.

Yes, indeed, but I do; the playermen are finer folks.

PINCHWIFE.

But you love none better than me?   70

MRS. PINCHWIFE.

You are mine own dear bud, and I know you; I hate a
stranger.

71. mine] Q1; my Q2–5, O.

PINCHWIFE.

Ay, my dear, you must love me only, and not be like the naughty town-women, who only hate their husbands and love every man else, love plays, visits, fine coaches, fine   75 clothes, fiddles, balls, treats, and so lead a wicked town-life.

MRS. PINCHWIFE.

Nay, if to enjoy all these things be a town-life, London is not so bad a place, dear.

PINCHWIFE.

How! If you love me, you must hate London.

ALITHEA [aside].

The fool has forbid me discovering to her the pleasures of   80 the town, and he is now setting her agog upon them himself.

MRS. PINCHWIFE.

But, husband, do the town-women love the playermen too?

PINCHWIFE.

Yes, I warrant you.

MRS. PINCHWIFE.

Ay, I warrant you.

PINCHWIFE.

Why, you do not, I hope?   85

MRS. PINCHWIFE.

No, no, bud; but why have we no playermen in the country?

PINCHWIFE.

Ha! —Mrs. Minx, ask me no more to go to a play.

MRS. PINCHWIFE.

Nay, why, love? I did not care for going; but when you forbid me, you make me, as 'twere, desire it.

ALITHEA (aside).

So 'twill be in other things, I warrant.   90

MRS. PINCHWIFE.

Pray let me go to a play, dear.

PINCHWIFE.

Hold your peace, I wo'not.

MRS. PINCHWIFE.

Why, love?

89. make me] *Q1, 3, 5, O;* make   92. your] *Q1–2, 4–5, O;* you *Q3. Q2, 4.*

PINCHWIFE.

Why, I'll tell you.

ALITHEA (*aside*).

Nay, if he tell her, she'll give him more cause to forbid her   95
that place.

MRS. PINCHWIFE.

Pray, why, dear?

PINCHWIFE.

First, you like the actors, and the gallants may like you.

MRS. PINCHWIFE.

What, a homely country girl? No, bud, nobody will like me.

PINCHWIFE.

I tell you, yes, they may.   100

MRS. PINCHWIFE.

No, no, you jest—I won't believe you, I will go.

PINCHWIFE.

I tell you then that one of the lewdest fellows in town, who
saw you there, told me he was in love with you.

MRS. PINCHWIFE.

Indeed! Who, who, pray who was't?

PINCHWIFE (*aside*).

I've gone too far, and slipped before I was aware. How   105
overjoyed she is!

MRS. PINCHWIFE.

Was it any Hampshire gallant, any of our neighbors? I
promise you, I am beholding to him.

PINCHWIFE.

I promise you, you lie; for he would but ruin you, as he has
done hundreds. He has no other love for women but that;   110
such as he look upon women, like basilisks, but to destroy
'em.

MRS. PINCHWIFE.

Ay, but if he loves me, why should he ruin me? Answer me
to that. Methinks he should not; I would do him no harm.

ALITHEA.

Ha, ha, ha!   115

PINCHWIFE.

'Tis very well; but I'll keep him from doing you any harm,
or me either.

---

111. *basilisks*] fabled serpents whose glance was fatal.

Enter Sparkish *and* Harcourt.

But here comes company; get you in, get you in.

MRS. PINCHWIFE.

But pray, husband, is he a pretty gentleman that loves me?

PINCHWIFE.

In, baggage, in. (*Thrusts her in; shuts the door.*) —[*Aside.*] 120
What, all the lewd libertines of the town brought to my
lodging by this easy coxcomb! 'Sdeath, I'll not suffer it.

SPARKISH.

Here, Harcourt, do you approve my choice? —[*To* Alithea.]
Dear little rogue, I told you I'd bring you acquainted with
all my friends, the wits, and—   125

(Harcourt *salutes her.*)

PINCHWIFE [*aside*].

Ay, they shall know her, as well as you yourself will, I
warrant you.

SPARKISH.

This is one of those, my pretty rogue, that are to dance at
your wedding tomorrow; and him you must bid welcome
ever to what you and I have.   130

PINCHWIFE (*aside*).

Monstrous!

SPARKISH.

Harcourt, how dost thou like her, faith? —Nay, dear, do
not look down; I should hate to have a wife of mine out of
countenance at anything.

PINCHWIFE [*aside*].

Wonderful!   135

SPARKISH.

Tell me, I say, Harcourt, how dost thou like her? Thou hast
stared upon her enough to resolve me.

HARCOURT.

So infinitely well that I could wish I had a mistress too,
that might differ from her in nothing but her love and
engagement to you.   140

ALITHEA.

Sir, Master Sparkish has often told me that his acquaintance
were all wits and railleurs, and now I find it.

---

142. *railleurs*] banterers.

SPARKISH.

No, by the universe, madam, he does not rally now; you
may believe him. I do assure you, he is the honestest,
worthiest, true-hearted gentleman—a man of such perfect 145
honor, he would say nothing to a lady he does not mean.

PINCHWIFE [aside].

Praising another man to his mistress!

HARCOURT.

Sir, you are so beyond expectation obliging that—

SPARKISH.

Nay, egad, I am sure you do admire her extremely; I see't
in your eyes. —He does admire you, madam. —By the 150
world, don't you?

HARCOURT.

Yes, above the world, or the most glorious part of it, her
whole sex; and till now I never thought I should have
envied you, or any man about to marry, but you have the
best excuse for marriage I ever knew.   155

ALITHEA.

Nay, now, sir, I'm satisfied you are of the society of the wits
and railleurs, since you cannot spare your friend, even when
he is but too civil to you; but the surest sign is, since you are
an enemy to marriage, for that, I hear, you hate as much
as business or bad wine.   160

HARCOURT.

Truly, madam, I never was an enemy to marriage till now,
because marriage was never an enemy to me before.

ALITHEA.

But why, sir, is marriage an enemy to you now? Because it
robs you of your friend here? For you look upon a friend
married as one gone into a monastery, that is, dead to the 165
world.

HARCOURT.

'Tis indeed because you marry him; I see, madam, you can
guess my meaning. I do confess heartily and openly, I wish
it were in my power to break the match; by heavens I
would.   170

161. never was] *Q1;* was never
Q2–5, O.

—31—

SPARKISH.

Poor Frank!

ALITHEA.

Would you be so unkind to me?

HARCOURT.

No, no, 'tis not because I would be unkind to you.

SPARKISH.

Poor Frank! No, gad, 'tis only his kindness to me.

PINCHWIFE (*aside*).

Great kindness to you indeed! Insensible fop, let a man make 175
love to his wife to his face!

SPARKISH.

Come, dear Frank, for all my wife there that shall be, thou
shalt enjoy me sometimes, dear rogue. By my honor, we
men of wit condole for our deceased brother in marriage as
much as for one dead in earnest. I think that was prettily 180
said of me, ha, Harcourt? But come, Frank, be not
melancholy for me.

HARCOURT.

No, I assure you I am not melancholy for you.

SPARKISH.

Prithee, Frank, dost think my wife that shall be there a fine
person? 185

HARCOURT.

I could gaze upon her till I became as blind as you are.

SPARKISH.

How, as I am? How?

HARCOURT.

Because you are a lover, and true lovers are blind, stock
blind.

SPARKISH.

True, true; but by the world, she has wit too, as well as 190
beauty. Go, go with her into a corner, and try if she has wit;
talk to her anything; she's bashful before me.

HARCOURT.

Indeed, if a woman wants wit in a corner, she has it nowhere.

ALITHEA (*aside to* Sparkish).

Sir, you dispose of me a little before your time—

SPARKISH.

Nay, nay, madam, let me have an earnest of your obedience, 195 or—go, go, madam—

(Harcourt *courts* Alithea *aside.*)

PINCHWIFE.

How, sir! If you are not concerned for the honor of a wife, I
am for that of a sister; he shall not debauch her. Be a pander
to your own wife, bring men to her, let 'em make love before
your face, thrust 'em into a corner together, then leave 'em 200
in private! Is this your town wit and conduct?

SPARKISH.

Ha, ha, ha! A silly wise rogue would make one laugh more
than a stark fool, ha, ha! I shall burst. Nay, you shall not
disturb 'em; I'll vex thee, by the world.

(*Struggles with* Pinchwife *to keep him from* Harcourt *and* Alithea.)

ALITHEA.

The writings are drawn, sir, settlements made; 'tis too late, 205
sir, and past all revocation.

HARCOURT.

Then so is my death.

ALITHEA.

I would not be unjust to him.

HARCOURT.

Then why to me so?

ALITHEA.

I have no obligation to you.   210

HARCOURT.

My love.

ALITHEA.

I had his before.

HARCOURT.

You never had it; he wants, you see, jealousy, the only
infallible sign of it.

ALITHEA.

Love proceeds from esteem; he cannot distrust my virtue; 215
besides, he loves me, or he would not marry me.

HARCOURT.

Marrying you is no more sign of his love than bribing your
woman, that he may marry you, is a sign of his generosity.
Marriage is rather a sign of interest than love; and he that
marries a fortune covets a mistress, not loves her. But if you 220
take marriage for a sign of love, take it from me immediately.

ALITHEA.

No, now you have put a scruple in my head; but, in short,
sir, to end our dispute, I must marry him, my reputation
would suffer in the world else.

HARCOURT.

No, if you do marry him, with your pardon, madam, your 225
reputation suffers in the world, and you would be thought
in necessity for a cloak.

ALITHEA.

Nay, now you are rude, sir. —Mr. Sparkish, pray come
hither, your friend here is very troublesome, and very loving.

HARCOURT (*aside to* Alithea).

Hold, hold!— 230

PINCHWIFE.

D'ye hear that?

SPARKISH.

Why, d'ye think I'll seem to be jealous, like a country
bumpkin?

PINCHWIFE.

No, rather be a cuckold, like a credulous cit.

HARCOURT.

Madam, you would not have been so little generous as to 235
have told him.

ALITHEA.

Yes, since you could be so little generous as to wrong him.

HARCOURT.

Wrong him! No man can do't, he's beneath an injury; a
bubble, a coward, a senseless idiot, a wretch so contemptible
to all the world but you that— 240

ALITHEA.

Hold, do not rail at him, for since he is like to be my
husband, I am resolved to like him. Nay, I think I am
obliged to tell him you are not his friend. —Master Sparkish,
Master Sparkish!

SPARKISH.

What, what? —Now, dear rogue, has not she wit? 245

---

234. *cit*] disparaging term for citizen; that is, not of gentry.
239. *bubble*] gullible fool.

HARCOURT (*speaks surlily*).

Not so much as I thought, and hoped she had.

ALITHEA.

Mr. Sparkish, do you bring people to rail at you?

HARCOURT.

Madam—

SPARKISH.

How! No, but if he does rail at me, 'tis but in jest, I warrant;
what we wits do for one another, and never take any notice 250
of it.

ALITHEA.

He spoke so scurrilously of you, I had no patience to hear
him; besides, he has been making love to me.

HARCOURT (*aside*).

True, damned, telltale woman!

SPARKISH.

Pshaw! to show his parts—we wits rail and make love often 255
but to show our parts; as we have no affections, so we have
no malice; we—

ALITHEA.

He said you were a wretch, below an injury.

SPARKISH.

Pshaw!

HARCOURT [*aside*].

Damned, senseless, impudent, virtuous jade! Well, since she 260
won't let me have her, she'll do as good, she'll make me hate
her.

ALITHEA.

A common bubble.

SPARKISH.

Pshaw!

ALITHEA.

A coward.   265

SPARKISH.

Pshaw, pshaw!

ALITHEA.

A senseless, driveling idiot.

SPARKISH.

How! Did he disparage my parts? Nay, then my honor's
concerned; I can't put up that, sir, by the world. Brother,

help me to kill him. —(*Aside.*)   I may draw now, since we 270
have the odds of him. 'Tis a good occasion, too, before my
mistress—   (*Offers to draw.*)

ALITHEA.

Hold, hold!

SPARKISH.

What, what?

ALITHEA (*aside*).

I must not let 'em kill the gentleman neither, for his kindness 275
to me; I am so far from hating him that I wish my gallant
had his person and understanding. Nay, if my honor—

SPARKISH.

I'll be thy death.

ALITHEA.

Hold, hold! Indeed, to tell the truth, the gentleman said
after all that what he spoke was but out of friendship to you. 280

SPARKISH.

How! say I am—I am a fool, that is, no wit, out of friendship
to me?

ALITHEA.

Yes, to try whether I was concerned enough for you, and
made love to me only to be satisfied of my virtue, for your
sake.   285

HARCOURT (*aside*).

Kind, however—

SPARKISH.

Nay, if it were so, my dear rogue, I ask thee pardon; but
why would not you tell me so, faith?

HARCOURT.

Because I did not think on't, faith.

SPARKISH.

Come, Horner does not come; Harcourt, let's be gone to the 290
new play. —Come, madam.

ALITHEA.

I will not go if you intend to leave me alone in the box and
run into the pit, as you use to do.

SPARKISH.

Pshaw! I'll leave Harcourt with you in the box to entertain

---

281. wit] *Q 1–4, O;* whit *Q 5.*   284. made] *Q 1–4, O;* make *Q 5.*

you, and that's as good; if I sat in the box, I should be 295
thought no judge, but of trimmings. —Come away,
Harcourt, lead her down.

Exeunt Sparkish, Harcourt, *and* Alithea.

PINCHWIFE.

Well, go thy ways, for the flower of the true town fops, such
as spend their estates before they come to 'em, and are
cuckolds before they're married. But let me go look to my 300
own freehold. —How!—

Enter My Lady Fidget, Mrs. Dainty Fidget, *and* Mrs. Squeamish.

LADY FIDGET.

Your servant, sir; where is your lady? We are come to wait
upon her to the new play.

PINCHWIFE.

New play!

LADY FIDGET.

And my husband will wait upon you presently.   305

PINCHWIFE (*aside*).

Damn your civility. —Madam, by no means; I will not see
Sir Jasper here till I have waited upon him at home; nor
shall my wife see you till she has waited upon your ladyship
at your lodgings.

LADY FIDGET.

Now we are here, sir—   310

PINCHWIFE.

No, madam.

MRS. DAINTY FIDGET.

Pray, let us see her.

MRS. SQUEAMISH.

We will not stir till we see her.

PINCHWIFE (*aside*).

A pox on you all!   (*Goes to the door, and returns.*) —She has
locked the door, and is gone abroad.   315

LADY FIDGET.

No, you have locked the door, and she's within.

306. (*aside*)] *Q 1–2, 4–5, O; om. Q 3.*

296. *trimmings*] clothes.

MRS. DAINTY FIDGET.

They told us below she was here.

PINCHWIFE [*aside*].

Will nothing do? —Well, it must out then. To tell you the truth, ladies, which I was afraid to let you know before, lest it might endanger your lives, my wife has just now the 320 smallpox come out upon her. Do not be frightened; but pray, be gone, ladies; you shall not stay here in danger of your lives; pray get you gone, ladies.

LADY FIDGET.

No, no, we have all had 'em.

MRS. SQUEAMISH.

Alack, alack!   325

MRS. DAINTY FIDGET.

Come, come, we must see how it goes with her; I understand the disease.

LADY FIDGET.

Come.

PINCHWIFE (*aside*).

Well, there is no being too hard for women at their own weapon, lying; therefore I'll quit the field.   330

Exit Pinchwife.

MRS. SQUEAMISH.

Here's an example of jealousy.

LADY FIDGET.

Indeed, as the world goes, I wonder there are no more jealous, since wives are so neglected.

MRS. DAINTY FIDGET.

Pshaw! as the world goes, to what end should they be jealous?   335

LADY FIDGET.

Foh! 'tis a nasty world.

MRS. SQUEAMISH.

That men of parts, great acquaintance, and quality should take up with and spend themselves and fortunes in keeping little playhouse creatures, foh!

LADY FIDGET.

Nay, that women of understanding, great acquaintance, 340 and good quality should fall a-keeping too of little creatures, foh!

MRS. SQUEAMISH.

Why, 'tis the men of quality's fault; they never visit women
of honor and reputation, as they used to do; and have not
so much as common civility for ladies of our rank, but use 345
us with the same indifferency and ill-breeding as if we were
all married to 'em.

LADY FIDGET.

She says true; 'tis an arrant shame women of quality
should be so slighted. Methinks birth—birth should go for
something; I have known men admired, courted, and 350
followed for their titles only.

MRS. SQUEAMISH.

Ay, one would think men of honor should not love, no
more than marry, out of their own rank.

MRS. DAINTY FIDGET.

Fie, fie upon 'em! They are come to think crossbreeding for
themselves best, as well as for their dogs and horses.   355

LADY FIDGET.

They are dogs and horses for't.

MRS. SQUEAMISH.

One would think, if not for love, for vanity a little.

MRS. DAINTY FIDGET.

Nay, they do satisfy their vanity upon us sometimes; and are
kind to us in their report, tell all the world they lie with us.

LADY FIDGET.

Damned rascals! That we should be only wronged by 'em; 360
to report a man has had a person, when he has not had a
person, is the greatest wrong in the whole world that can
be done to a person.

MRS. SQUEAMISH.

Well, 'tis an arrant shame noble persons should be so
wronged and neglected.   365

LADY FIDGET.

But still 'tis an arranter shame for a noble person to neglect
her own honor, and defame her own noble person with
little inconsiderable fellows, foh!

MRS. DAINTY FIDGET.

I suppose the crime against our honor is the same with a

343. women] *Q1–4, O;* woman *Q5.*

man of quality as with another.   370

LADY FIDGET.

How! No, sure, the man of quality is likest one's husband,
and therefore the fault should be the less.

MRS. DAINTY FIDGET.

But then the pleasure should be the less.

LADY FIDGET.

Fie, fie, fie, for shame, sister! Whither shall we ramble?
Be continent in your discourse, or I shall hate you.   375

MRS. DAINTY FIDGET.

Besides, an intrigue is so much the more notorious for the
man's quality.

MRS. SQUEAMISH.

'Tis true, nobody takes notice of a private man, and
therefore with him 'tis more secret, and the crime's the
less when 'tis not known.   380

LADY FIDGET.

You say true; i'faith, I think you are in the right on't. 'Tis
not an injury to a husband till it be an injury to our honors;
so that a woman of honor loses no honor with a private
person; and to say truth—

MRS. DAINTY FIDGET (*apart to* [Mrs.] Squeamish).

So, the little fellow is grown a private person—with her—   385

LADY FIDGET.

But still my dear, dear honor.

Enter Sir Jasper, Horner, Dorilant.

SIR JASPER FIDGET.

Ay, my dear, dear of honor, thou hast still so much honor
in thy mouth—

HORNER (*aside*).

That she has none elsewhere.

LADY FIDGET.

Oh, what d'ye mean to bring in these upon us?   390

MRS. DAINTY FIDGET.

Foh! these are as bad as wits.

MRS. SQUEAMISH.

Foh!

382. honors] *Q 1–4, O;* honor *Q 5.*

LADY FIDGET.

Let us leave the room.

SIR JASPER FIDGET.

Stay, stay; faith, to tell you the naked truth—

LADY FIDGET.

Fie, Sir Jasper! Do not use that word "naked."   395

SIR JASPER FIDGET.

Well, well, in short, I have business at Whitehall, and cannot go to the play with you, therefore would have you go—

LADY FIDGET.

With those two to a play?

SIR JASPER FIDGET.

No, not with t'other, but with Mr. Horner; there can be   400 no more scandal to go with him than with Mr. Tattle, or Master Limberham.

LADY FIDGET.

With that nasty fellow! No—no!

SIR JASPER FIDGET.

Nay, prithee, dear, hear me.

(*Whispers to* Lady Fidget.)

HORNER.

Ladies—   405

(Horner, Dorilant *drawing near* [Mrs.] Squeamish *and* [Mrs.] Dainty.)

MRS. DAINTY FIDGET.

Stand off.

MRS. SQUEAMISH.

Do not approach us.

MRS. DAINTY FIDGET.

You herd with the wits, you are obscenity all over.

MRS. SQUEAMISH.

And I would as soon look upon a picture of Adam and Eve, without fig leaves, as any of you, if I could help it; therefore   410 keep off, and do not make us sick.

DORILANT.

What a devil are these?

395. that word] *Q1–4, O;* the word *Q5.*

401–402. *Mr. Tattle, or Master Limberham*] common names for harmless gallants, later used by Congreve and by Dryden for their characters.

HORNER.

Why, these are pretenders to honor, as critics to wit, only by
censuring others; and as every raw, peevish, out-of-
humored, affected, dull, tea-drinking, arithmetical fop sets 415
up for a wit by railing at men of sense, so these for honor
by railing at the Court, and ladies of as great honor as
quality.

SIR JASPER FIDGET.

Come, Mr. Horner, I must desire you to go with these ladies
to the play, sir. 420

HORNER.

I, sir!

SIR JASPER FIDGET.

Ay, ay, come, sir.

HORNER.

I must beg your pardon, sir, and theirs; I will not be seen in
women's company in public again for the world.

SIR JASPER FIDGET.

Ha, ha! strange aversion! 425

MRS. SQUEAMISH.

No, he's for women's company in private.

SIR JASPER FIDGET.

He—poor man—he! Ha, ha, ha!

MRS. DAINTY FIDGET.

'Tis a greater shame amongst lewd fellows to be seen in
virtuous women's company than for the women to be seen
with them. 430

HORNER.

Indeed, madam, the time was I only hated virtuous women,
but now I hate the other too; I beg your pardon, ladies.

LADY FIDGET.

You are very obliging, sir, because we would not be troubled
with you.

SIR JASPER FIDGET.

In sober sadness, he shall go. 435

DORILANT.

Nay, if he wo'not, I am ready to wait upon the ladies; and I
think I am the fitter man.

---

415. *arithmetical*] exact, precise.

SIR JASPER FIDGET.

You, sir, no, I thank you for that—Master Horner is a
privileged man amongst the virtuous ladies; 'twill be a great
while before you are so, he, he, he! He's my wife's gallant, 440
he, he, he! No, pray withdraw, sir, for as I take it, the
virtuous ladies have no business with you.

DORILANT.

And I am sure he can have none with them. 'Tis strange a
man can't come amongst virtuous women now but upon
the same terms as men are admitted into the Great Turk's 445
seraglio; but heavens keep me from being an ombre
player with 'em! But where is Pinchwife?

Exit Dorilant.

SIR JASPER FIDGET.

Come, come, man; what, avoid the sweet society of womankind? that sweet, soft, gentle, tame, noble creature, woman,
made for man's companion— 450

HORNER.

So is that soft, gentle, tame, and more noble creature a
spaniel, and has all their tricks—can fawn, lie down, suffer
beating, and fawn the more; barks at your friends when
they come to see you; makes your bed hard; gives you fleas,
and the mange sometimes. And all the difference is, the 455
spaniel's the more faithful animal, and fawns but upon one
master.

SIR JASPER FIDGET.

He, he, he!

MRS. SQUEAMISH.

Oh, the rude beast!

MRS. DAINTY FIDGET.

Insolent brute! 460

LADY FIDGET.

Brute! Stinking, mortified, rotten French wether, to dare—

SIR JASPER FIDGET.

Hold, an't please your ladyship. —For shame, Master
Horner, your mother was a woman. —(*Aside.*) Now shall

---

445. *Great Turk's*] Turkish sultan's.
461. *French wether*] castrated ram, but here a man made impotent by
French pox.

I never reconcile 'em. —[*Aside to* Lady Fidget.] Hark
you, madam, take my advice in your anger. You know you 465
often want one to make up your drolling pack of ombre
players; and you may cheat him easily, for he's an ill
gamester, and consequently loves play. Besides, you know,
you have but two old civil gentlemen, with stinking breaths
too, to wait upon you abroad; take in the third into your 470
service. The other are but crazy; and a lady should have a
supernumerary gentleman-usher, as a supernumerary
coach-horse, lest sometimes you should be forced to stay at
home.

LADY FIDGET.

But are you sure he loves play, and has money?   475

SIR JASPER FIDGET.

He loves play as much as you, and has money as much as I.

LADY FIDGET.

Then I am contented to make him pay for his scurrility;
money makes up in a measure all other wants in men.
—(*Aside.*)   Those whom we cannot make hold for gallants,
we make fine.   480

SIR JASPER FIDGET (*aside*).

So, so; now to mollify, to wheedle him. —Master Horner,
will you never keep civil company? Methinks 'tis time now,
since you are only fit for them. Come, come, man, you must
e'en fall to visiting our wives, eating at our tables, drinking
tea with our virtuous relations after dinner, dealing cards to 485
'em, reading plays and gazettes to 'em, picking fleas out of
their shocks for 'em, collecting receipts, new songs, women,
pages, and footmen for 'em.

HORNER.

I hope they'll afford me better employment, sir.

SIR JASPER FIDGET.

He, he, he! 'Tis fit you know your work before you come 490
into your place; and since you are unprovided of a lady to
flatter and a good house to eat at, pray frequent mine, and

---

466. *drolling*] comic, quaint.
471. *crazy*] unsound.
480. *fine*] pay.
487. *shocks*] poodles.

call my wife mistress, and she shall call you gallant, according
to the custom.

SIR JASPER FIDGET.

HORNER.

Who, I? 495

SIR JASPER FIDGET.

Faith, thou shalt for my sake; come, for my sake only.

HORNER.

For your sake—

SIR JASPER FIDGET [*to* Lady Fidget].

Come, come, here's a gamester for you; let him be a little
familiar sometimes; nay, what if a little rude? Gamesters
may be rude with ladies, you know. 500

LADY FIDGET.

Yes, losing gamesters have a privilege with women.

HORNER.

I always thought the contrary, that the winning gamester
had most privilege with women; for when you have lost
your money to a man, you'll lose anything you have, all
you have, they say, and he may use you as he pleases. 505

SIR JASPER FIDGET.

He, he, he! Well, win or lose, you shall have your liberty
with her.

LADY FIDGET.

As he behaves himself; and for your sake I'll give him
admittance and freedom.

HORNER.

All sorts of freedom, madam? 510

SIR JASPER FIDGET.

Ay, ay, ay, all sorts of freedom thou canst take, and so go to
her, begin thy new employment; wheedle her, jest with her,
and be better acquainted one with another.

HORNER (*aside*).

I think I know her already, therefore may venture with her,
my secret for hers. 515

(Horner *and* Lady Fidget *whisper.*)

SIR JASPER FIDGET.

Sister, cuz, I have provided an innocent playfellow for you
there.

514. venture] *Q2–5, O;* venter *Q1.*

MRS. DAINTY FIDGET.

Who, he!

MRS. SQUEAMISH.

There's a playfellow indeed!

SIR JASPER FIDGET.

Yes, sure; what, he is good enough to play at cards, blind-   520
man's buff, or the fool with sometimes.

MRS. SQUEAMISH.

Foh! we'll have no such playfellows.

MRS. DAINTY FIDGET.

No, sir, you shan't choose playfellows for us, we thank you.

SIR JASPER FIDGET.

Nay, pray hear me.

(*Whispering to them.*)

LADY FIDGET [*aside to* Horner].

But, poor gentleman, could you be so generous, so truly a   525
man of honor, as for the sakes of us women of honor, to cause
yourself to be reported no man? No man! And to suffer
yourself the greatest shame that could fall upon a man, that
none might fall upon us women by your conversation?
But indeed, sir, as perfectly, perfectly, the same man as   530
before your going into France, sir? as perfectly, perfectly,
sir?

HORNER.

As perfectly, perfectly, madam. Nay, I scorn you should
take my word; I desire to be tried only, madam.

LADY FIDGET.

Well, that's spoken again like a man of honor; all men of   535
honor desire to come to the test. But, indeed, generally you
men report such things of yourselves, one does not know how
or whom to believe; and it is come to that pass we dare not
take your words, no more than your tailor's, without some
staid servant of yours be bound with you. But I have so   540
strong a faith in your honor, dear, dear, noble sir, that I'd
forfeit mine for yours at any time, dear sir.

HORNER.

No, madam, you should not need to forfeit it for me; I have

540. staid] *Q1–2, 4–5, O;* maid *Q3.*

-46-

given you security already to save you harmless, my late
reputation being so well known in the world, madam.   545

LADY FIDGET.

But if upon any future falling out, or upon a suspicion of my
taking the trust out of your hands, to employ some other,
you yourself should betray your trust, dear sir? I mean, if
you'll give me leave to speak obscenely, you might tell, dear
sir.   550

HORNER.

If I did, nobody would believe me; the reputation of
impotency is as hardly recovered again in the world as that
of cowardice, dear madam.

LADY FIDGET.

Nay then, as one may say, you may do your worst, dear,
dear sir.   555

SIR JASPER FIDGET.

Come, is your ladyship reconciled to him yet? Have you
agreed on matters? For I must be gone to Whitehall.

LADY FIDGET.

Why, indeed, Sir Jasper, Master Horner is a thousand,
thousand times a better man than I thought him. Cousin
Squeamish, Sister Dainty, I can name him now; truly, not 560
long ago, you know, I thought his very name obscenity, and
I would as soon have lain with him as have named him.

SIR JASPER FIDGET.

Very likely, poor madam.

MRS. DAINTY FIDGET.

I believe it.

MRS. SQUEAMISH.

No doubt on't.   565

SIR JASPER FIDGET.

Well, well—that your ladyship is as virtuous as any she,
I know, and him all the town knows—he, he, he! Therefore,
now you like him, get you gone to your business together;
go, go to your business, I say, pleasure, whilst I go to my
pleasure, business.   570

LADY FIDGET.

Come, then, dear gallant.

---

549. *obscenely*] openly.

HORNER.

Come away, my dearest mistress.

SIR JASPER FIDGET.

So, so; why, 'tis as I'd have it.

Exit Sir Jasper.

HORNER.

And as I'd have it.

LADY FIDGET.

Who for his business from his wife will run,   575
Takes the best care to have her business done.

Exeunt omnes.

[III.i]   Alithea *and* Mrs. Pinchwife.

ALITHEA.

Sister, what ails you? You are grown melancholy.

MRS. PINCHWIFE.

Would it not make anyone melancholy, to see you go every
day fluttering about abroad, whilst I must stay at home like
a poor, lonely, sullen bird in a cage?

ALITHEA.

Ay, sister, but you came young and just from the nest to   5
your cage, so that I thought you liked it, and could be as
cheerful in't as others that took their flight themselves early,
and are hopping abroad in the open air.

MRS. PINCHWIFE.

Nay, I confess I was quiet enough till my husband told me
what pure lives the London ladies live abroad, with their   10
dancing, meetings, and junketings, and dressed every day in
their best gowns; and I warrant you, play at ninepins every
day of the week, so they do.

Enter Mr. Pinchwife.

PINCHWIFE.

Come, what's here to do? You are putting the town pleasures
in her head, and setting her a-longing.   15

15. setting] *Q1–2, 4–5, O;* set *Q3.*

___

10. *pure*] fine.

ALITHEA.

Yes, after ninepins; you suffer none to give her those longings, you mean, but yourself.

PINCHWIFE.

I tell her of the vanities of the town like a confessor.

ALITHEA.

A confessor! Just such a confessor as he that, by forbidding a silly ostler to grease the horse's teeth, taught him to do't.   20

PINCHWIFE.

Come, Mistress Flippant, good precepts are lost when bad examples are still before us; the liberty you take abroad makes her hanker after it, and out of humor at home. Poor wretch! she desired not to come to London; I would bring her.   25

ALITHEA.

Very well.

PINCHWIFE.

She has been this week in town, and never desired, till this afternoon, to go abroad.

ALITHEA.

Was she not at a play yesterday?

PINCHWIFE.

Yes, but she ne'er asked me; I was myself the cause of her   30 going.

ALITHEA.

Then, if she ask you again, you are the cause of her asking, and not my example.

PINCHWIFE.

Well, tomorrow night I shall be rid of you; and the next day, before 'tis light, she and I'll be rid of the town, and my   35 dreadful apprehensions. —[*To* Mrs. Pinchwife.]   Come, be not melancholy, for thou shalt go into the country after tomorrow, dearest.

ALITHEA.

Great comfort!

MRS. PINCHWIFE.

Pish! what d'ye tell me of the country for?   40

---

20. *silly*] ignorant.

PINCHWIFE.

How's this! What, pish at the country?

MRS. PINCHWIFE.

Let me alone, I am not well.

PINCHWIFE.

Oh, if that be all—what ails my dearest?

MRS. PINCHWIFE.

Truly I don't know; but I have not been well since you told
me there was a gallant at the play in love with me.   45

PINCHWIFE.

Ha!—

ALITHEA.

That's by my example too!

PINCHWIFE.

Nay, if you are not well, but are so concerned because a lewd
fellow chanced to lie, and say he liked you, you'll make me
sick too.   50

MRS. PINCHWIFE.

Of what sickness?

PINCHWIFE.

Oh, of that which is worse than the plague, jealousy.

MRS. PINCHWIFE.

Pish, you jeer! I'm sure there's no such disease in our
receipt-book at home.

PINCHWIFE.

No, thou never met'st with it, poor innocent. —(*Aside.*)   55
Well, if thou cuckold me, 'twill be my own fault—for
cuckolds and bastards are generally makers of their own
fortune.

MRS. PINCHWIFE.

Well, but pray, bud, let's go to a play tonight.

PINCHWIFE.

'Tis just done, she comes from it. But why are you so eager   60
to see a play?

MRS. PINCHWIFE.

Faith, dear, not that I care one pin for their talk there; but
I like to look upon the playermen, and would see, if I could,
the gallant you say loves me; that's all, dear bud.

PINCHWIFE.

Is that all, dear bud?   65

ALITHEA.

This proceeds from my example.

MRS. PINCHWIFE.

But if the play be done, let's go abroad, however, dear bud.

PINCHWIFE.

Come, have a little patience, and thou shalt go into the country on Friday.

MRS. PINCHWIFE.

Therefore I would see first some sights, to tell my neighbors   70
of. Nay, I will go abroad, that's once.

ALITHEA.

I'm the cause of this desire too.

PINCHWIFE.

But now I think on't, who was the cause of Horner's coming to my lodging today? That was you.

ALITHEA.

No, you, because you would not let him see your handsome   75
wife out of your lodging.

MRS. PINCHWIFE.

Why, O Lord! did the gentleman come hither to see me indeed?

PINCHWIFE.

No, no. —You are not the cause of that damned question too, Mistress Alithea? —(*Aside.*)   Well, she's in the right of   80
it. He is in love with my wife—and comes after her—'tis so—but I'll nip his love in the bud; lest he should follow us into the country, and break his chariot-wheel near our house on purpose for an excuse to come to't. But I think I know the town.   85

MRS. PINCHWIFE.

Come, pray, bud, let's go abroad before 'tis late; for I will go, that's flat and plain.

PINCHWIFE (*aside*).

So! the obstinacy already of a town-wife, and I must, whilst she's here, humor her like one. —Sister, how shall we do,

73. who] *Q1*; who, who *Q2–5, O.*   88. a town-wife] *Q1*; the townwife
79. the cause] *Q4–5, O*; cause   *Q2–5, O.*
Q1–3.

that she may not be seen or known?   90
ALITHEA.

Let her put on her mask.
PINCHWIFE.

Pshaw! A mask makes people but the more inquisitive, and
is as ridiculous a disguise as a stage-beard; her shape, stature,
habit will be known. And if we should meet with Horner,
he would be sure to take acquaintance with us, must wish   95
her joy, kiss her, talk to her, leer upon her, and the devil
and all. No, I'll not use her to a mask, 'tis dangerous; for
masks have made more cuckolds than the best faces that
ever were known.
ALITHEA.

How will you do then?   100
MRS. PINCHWIFE.

Nay, shall we go? The Exchange will be shut, and I have
a mind to see that.
PINCHWIFE.

So—I have it—I'll dress her up in the suit we are to carry
down to her brother, little sir James; nay, I understand
the town tricks. Come, let's go dress her. A mask! No—a 105
woman masked, like a covered dish, gives a man curiosity
and appetite, when, it may be, uncovered, 'twould turn his
stomach; no, no.
ALITHEA.

Indeed your comparison is something a greasy one. But I
had a gentle gallant used to say, "A beauty masked, like 110
the sun in eclipse, gathers together more gazers than if it
shined out."

Exeunt.

[III.ii]   *The scene changes to the New Exchange.*
                    Enter Horner, Harcourt, Dorilant.

DORILANT.

Engaged to women, and not sup with us?
HORNER.

Ay, a pox on 'em all!
HARCOURT.

You were much a more reasonable man in the morning,

and had as noble resolutions against 'em as a widower of a
week's liberty.   5

DORILANT.

Did I ever think to see you keep company with women in
vain?

HORNER.

In vain! No—'tis, since I can't love 'em, to be revenged on
'em.

HARCOURT.

Now your sting is gone, you looked in the box, amongst all   10
those women, like a drone in the hive, all upon you; shoved
and ill-used by 'em all, and thrust from one side to t'other.

DORILANT.

Yet he must be buzzing amongst 'em still, like other old
beetle-headed, liquorish drones. Avoid 'em, and hate 'em
as they hate you.   15

HORNER.

Because I do hate 'em, and would hate 'em yet more, I'll
frequent 'em; you may see by marriage, nothing makes a
man hate a woman more than her constant conversation.
In short, I converse with 'em, as you do with rich fools, to
laugh at 'em and use 'em ill.   20

DORILANT.

But I would no more sup with women, unless I could lie
with 'em, than sup with a rich coxcomb, unless I could
cheat him.

HORNER.

Yes, I have known thee sup with a fool for his drinking;
if he could set out your hand that way only, you were   25
satisfied, and if he were a wine-swallowing mouth 'twas
enough.

HARCOURT.

Yes, a man drinks often with a fool, as he tosses with a
marker, only to keep his hand in ure. But do the ladies
drink?   30

HORNER.

Yes, sir, and I shall have the pleasure at least of laying 'em

---

29. *marker*] scorekeeper.   29. *ure*] practice.

flat with a bottle, and bring as much scandal that way upon
'em as formerly t'other.

HARCOURT.

Perhaps you may prove as weak a brother amongst 'em that
way as t'other.   35

DORILANT.

Foh! drinking with women is as unnatural as scolding with
'em; but 'tis a pleasure of decayed fornicators, and the
basest way of quenching love.

HARCOURT.

Nay, 'tis drowning love instead of quenching it. But leave
us for civil women too!   40

DORILANT.

Ay, when he can't be the better for 'em. We hardly pardon
a man that leaves his friend for a wench, and that's a pretty
lawful call.

HORNER.

Faith, I would not leave you for 'em, if they would not
drink.   45

DORILANT.

Who would disappoint his company at Lewis's for a
gossiping?

HARCOURT.

Foh! Wine and women, good apart, together as nauseous as
sack and sugar. But hark you, sir, before you go, a little of
your advice; an old maimed general, when unfit for action,   50
is fittest for counsel. I have other designs upon women than
eating and drinking with them. I am in love with Sparkish's
mistress, whom he is to marry tomorrow. Now how shall I
get her?

Enter Sparkish, *looking about.*

HORNER.

Why, here comes one will help you to her.   55

HARCOURT.

He! He, I tell you, is my rival, and will hinder my love.

HORNER.

No, a foolish rival and a jealous husband assist their rival's

---

34–35. that way as] *Q1–4, O;* as
formerly *Q5.*

designs; for they are sure to make their women hate them, which is the first step to their love for another man.

HARCOURT.

But I cannot come near his mistress but in his company.   60

HORNER.

Still the better for you, for fools are most easily cheated when they themselves are accessories; and he is to be bubbled of his mistress, as of his money, the common mistress, by keeping him company.

SPARKISH.

Who is that, that is to be bubbled? Faith, let me snack,   65
I han't met with a bubble since Christmas. Gad, I think bubbles are like their brother woodcocks, go out with the cold weather.

HARCOURT (*apart to* Horner).

A pox! he did not hear all, I hope.

SPARKISH.

Come, you bubbling rogues you, where do we sup? —Oh,   70
Harcourt, my mistress tells me you have been making fierce love to her all the play long, ha, ha! But I—

HARCOURT.

I make love to her?

SPARKISH.

Nay, I forgive thee; for I think I know thee, and I know her, but I am sure I know myself.   75

HARCOURT.

Did she tell you so? I see all women are like these of the Exchange, who, to enhance the price of their commodities, report to their fond customers offers which were never made 'em.

HORNER.

Ay, women are as apt to tell before the intrigue as men after   80
it, and so show themselves the vainer sex. But hast thou a mistress, Sparkish? 'Tis as hard for me to believe it as that thou ever hadst a bubble, as you bragged just now.

80. as apt] *Q1;* apt *Q2–5, O.*

62. *bubbled*] gulled.
65. *snack*] share.
67. *woodcocks*] simpletons.

SPARKISH.

Oh, your servant, sir; are you at your raillery, sir? But we
were some of us beforehand with you today at the play.   85
The wits were something bold with you, sir; did you not
hear us laugh?

HORNER.

Yes, but I thought you had gone to plays to laugh at the
poet's wit, not at your own.

SPARKISH.

Your servant, sir; no, I thank you. Gad, I go to a play as to   90
a country treat; I carry my own wine to one, and my own wit
to t'other, or else I'm sure I should not be merry at either.
And the reason why we are so often louder than the players
is because we think we speak more wit, and so become the
poet's rivals in his audience. For to tell you the truth, we   95
hate the silly rogues; nay, so much that we find fault even
with their bawdy upon the stage, whilst we talk nothing
else in the pit as loud.

HORNER.

But why shouldst thou hate the silly poets? Thou hast too
much wit to be one, and they, like whores, are only hated by   100
each other; and thou dost scorn writing, I'm sure.

SPARKISH.

Yes, I'd have you to know I scorn writing; but women,
women, that make men do all foolish things, make 'em
write songs too; everybody does it. 'Tis even as common with
lovers as playing with fans; and you can no more help   105
rhyming to your Phyllis than drinking to your Phyllis.

HARCOURT.

Nay, poetry in love is no more to be avoided than jealousy.

DORILANT.

But the poets damned your songs, did they?

SPARKISH.

Damn the poets! They turned 'em into burlesque, as they
call it. That burlesque is a hocus-pocus trick they have got,   110
which, by the virtue of *hictius doctius*, *topsy-turvy*, they make a
wise and witty man in the world a fool upon the stage, you

85. were] *Q1;* are *Q2–5, O.*

know not how; and 'tis therefore I hate 'em too, for I know
not but it may be my own case; for they'll put a man into a
play for looking asquint. Their predecessors were contented 115
to make serving-men only their stage-fools, but these rogues
must have gentlemen, with a pox to 'em, nay, knights. And,
indeed, you shall hardly see a fool upon the stage but he's a
knight; and to tell you the truth, they have kept me these
six years from being a knight in earnest, for fear of being 120
knighted in a play, and dubbed a fool.

DORILANT.

Blame 'em not; they must follow their copy, the age.

HARCOURT.

But why shouldst thou be afraid of being in a play, who
expose yourself every day in the playhouses, and as public
places?   125

HORNER.

'Tis but being on the stage, instead of standing on a bench in
the pit.

DORILANT.

Don't you give money to painters to draw you like? And
are you afraid of your pictures at length in a playhouse,
where all your mistresses may see you?   130

SPARKISH.

A pox! Painters don't draw the smallpox or pimples in one's
face. Come, damn all your silly authors whatever, all books
and booksellers, by the world, and all readers, courteous or
uncourteous.

HARCOURT.

But who comes here, Sparkish?   135

Enter Mr. Pinchwife, *and his wife in man's clothes,* Alithea, Lucy *her maid.*

SPARKISH.

Oh, hide me! There's my mistress too.
                        (Sparkish *hides himself behind* Harcourt.)

HARCOURT.

She sees you.

122. their] *Q 1–4, O;* in their *Q 5.*   124. as] *Q 1–2;* at *Q 3–5, O.*

124. *as*] equally.

SPARKISH.

But I will not see her. 'Tis time to go to Whitehall, and I
must not fail the drawing room.

HARCOURT.

Pray, first carry me, and reconcile me to her.   140

SPARKISH.

Another time; faith, the King will have supped.

HARCOURT.

Not with the worse stomach for thy absence; thou art one of
those fools that think their attendance at the King's meals as
necessary as his physicians', when you are more troublesome
to him than his doctors, or his dogs.   145

SPARKISH.

Pshaw! I know my interest, sir; prithee hide me.

HORNER.

Your servant, Pinchwife. —What, he knows us not!

PINCHWIFE (*to his wife aside*).

Come along.

MRS. PINCHWIFE.

Pray, have you any ballads? Give me sixpenny worth.

CLASP.

We have no ballads.   150

MRS. PINCHWIFE.

Then give me *Covent Garden Drollery*, and a play or two—Oh,
here's *Tarugo's Wiles*, and *The Slighted Maiden*; I'll have
them.

PINCHWIFE (*apart to her*).

No, plays are not for your reading. Come along; will you
discover yourself?   155

HORNER.

Who is that pretty youth with him, Sparkish?

SPARKISH.

I believe his wife's brother, because he's something like her;
but I never saw her but once.

HORNER.

Extremely handsome; I have seen a face like it too. Let us

---

151. *Covent Garden Drollery*] collection of songs and poems (1672).
152. *Tarugo's Wiles*] comedy by Sir Thomas St. Serfe (1667).
152. *The Slighted Maid*] comedy by Sir Robert Stapylton (1663).

follow 'em.   160

Exeunt Pinchwife, Mrs. Pinchwife. Alithea, Lucy, Horner, Dorilant *following them.*

HARCOURT.

Come, Sparkish, your mistress saw you, and will be angry you go not to her. Besides, I would fain be reconciled to her, which none but you can do, dear friend.

SPARKISH.

Well, that's a better reason, dear friend. I would not go near her now, for hers or my own sake, but I can deny you 165 nothing; for though I have known thee a great while, never go, if I do not love thee as well as a new acquaintance.

HARCOURT.

I am obliged to you indeed, dear friend. I would be well with her, only to be well with thee still; for these ties to wives usually dissolve all ties to friends. I would be contented she 170 should enjoy you a-nights, but I would have you to myself a-days, as I have had, dear friend.

SPARKISH.

And thou shalt enjoy me a-days, dear, dear friend, never stir; and I'll be divorced from her sooner than from thee. Come along.   175

HARCOURT *(aside)*.

So, we are hard put to't when we make our rival our procurer; but neither she nor her brother would let me come near her now. When all's done, a rival is the best cloak to steal to a mistress under, without suspicion; and when we have once got to her as we desire, we throw him off like 180 other cloaks.

                    Exit Sparkish, *and* Harcourt *following him.*

        Re-enter Mr. Pinchwife, Mrs. Pinchwife *in man's clothes.*

PINCHWIFE *(to* Alithea *[off-stage])*.

Sister, if you will not go, we must leave you. —*(Aside.)* The fool her gallant and she will muster up all the young saunterers of this place, and they will leave their dear

173. dear, dear] *Q 1–2, 4, O;* dear
Q 3, 5.

---

174. *stir]* be upset.

seamstresses to follow us. What a swarm of cuckolds, and 185
cuckold-makers, are here! —Come, let's be gone, Mistress
Margery.

MRS. PINCHWIFE.

Don't you believe that, I han't half my bellyfull of sights yet.

PINCHWIFE.

Then walk this way.

MRS. PINCHWIFE.

Lord, what a power of brave signs are here! Stay—the 190
Bull's-Head, the Ram's-Head, and the Stag's-Head, dear—

PINCHWIFE.

Nay, if every husband's proper sign here were visible, they
would be all alike.

MRS. PINCHWIFE.

What d'ye mean by that, bud?

PINCHWIFE.

'Tis no matter—no matter, bud.   195

MRS. PINCHWIFE.

Pray tell me; nay, I will know.

PINCHWIFE.

They would be all bulls', stags', and rams' heads.

                    Exeunt Mr. Pinchwife, Mrs. Pinchwife.

Re-enter Sparkish, Harcourt, Alithea, Lucy, *at t'other door.*

SPARKISH.

Come, dear madam, for my sake you shall be reconciled to
him.

ALITHEA.

For your sake I hate him.   200

HARCOURT.

That's something too cruel, madam, to hate me for his sake.

SPARKISH.

Ay indeed, madam, too, too cruel to me, to hate my friend
for my sake.

ALITHEA.

I hate him because he is your enemy; and you ought to
hate him too, for making love to me, if you love me.   205

---

192. *husband's proper sign*] cuckold's horns.
197.2. *at t'other door*] there were two doors on each side of the stage.

SPARKISH.

That's a good one; I hate a man for loving you! If he did
love you, 'tis but what he can't help; and 'tis your fault, not
his, if he admires you. I hate a man for being of my opinion!
I'll ne'er do't, by the world.

ALITHEA.

Is it for your honor or mine, to suffer a man to make love to   210
me, who am to marry you tomorrow?

SPARKISH.

Is it for your honor or mine, to have me jealous? That he
makes love to you is a sign you are handsome; and that I am
not jealous is a sign you are virtuous. That, I think, is for
your honor.   215

ALITHEA.

But 'tis your honor too I am concerned for.

HARCOURT.

But why, dearest madam, will you be more concerned for
his honor than he is himself? Let his honor alone, for my
sake and his. He, he has no honor—

SPARKISH.

How's that?   220

HARCOURT.

But what my dear friend can guard himself.

SPARKISH.

O ho—that's right again.

HARCOURT.

Your care of his honor argues his neglect of it, which is no
honor to my dear friend here; therefore once more, let his
honor go which way it will, dear madam.   225

SPARKISH.

Ay, ay, were it for my honor to marry a woman whose virtue
I suspected, and could not trust her in a friend's hands?

ALITHEA.

Are you not afraid to lose me?

HARCOURT.

He afraid to lose you, madam! No, no—you may see how
the most estimable and most glorious creature in the world   230
is valued by him. Will you not see it?

SPARKISH.

Right, honest Frank, I have that noble value for her that I

cannot be jealous of her.

ALITHEA.

You mistake him, he means you care not for me, nor who
has me. 235

SPARKISH.

Lord, madam, I see you are jealous. Will you wrest a poor
man's meaning from his words?

ALITHEA.

You astonish me, sir, with your want of jealousy.

SPARKISH.

And you make me giddy, madam, with your jealousy and
fears, and virtue and honor. Gad, I see virtue makes a 240
woman as troublesome as a little reading or learning.

ALITHEA.

Monstrous!

LUCY (behind).

Well, to see what easy husbands these women of quality can
meet with; a poor chambermaid can never have such
lady-like luck. Besides, he's thrown away upon her; she'll 245
make no use of her fortune, her blessing; none to a gentleman
for a pure cuckold, for it requires good breeding to be a
cuckold.

ALITHEA.

I tell you then plainly, he pursues me to marry me.

SPARKISH.

Pshaw! 250

HARCOURT.

Come, madam, you see you strive in vain to make him
jealous of me; my dear friend is the kindest creature in the
world to me.

SPARKISH.

Poor fellow.

HARCOURT.

But his kindness only is not enough for me, without your 255
favor; your good opinion, dear madam, 'tis that must
perfect my happiness. Good gentleman, he believes all I

---

255. only] Q1–2, 4–5, O; om. Q3.

236. jealous] vehement in feeling.

say; would you would do so. Jealous of me! I would not
wrong him nor you for the world.

SPARKISH.

Look you there; hear him, hear him, and do not walk away so.   260

(Alithea *walks carelessly to and fro.*)

HARCOURT.

I love you, madam, so—

SPARKISH.

How's that! Nay—now you begin to go too far indeed.

HARCOURT.

So much, I confess, I say I love you, that I would not have
you miserable, and cast yourself away upon so unworthy and
inconsiderable a thing as what you see here.   265

(*Clapping his hand on his breast, points at Sparkish.*)

SPARKISH.

No, faith, I believe thou wouldst not; now his meaning is
plain. But I knew before thou wouldst not wrong me nor her.

HARCOURT.

No, no, heavens forbid the glory of her sex should fall so low
as into the embraces of such a contemptible wretch, the last
of mankind—my dear friend here—I injure him!   270

(*Embracing* Sparkish.)

ALITHEA.

Very well.

SPARKISH.

No, no, dear friend, I knew it. —Madam, you see he will
rather wrong himself than me, in giving himself such names.

ALITHEA.

Do not you understand him yet?

SPARKISH.

Yes, how modestly he speaks of himself, poor fellow.   275

ALITHEA.

Methinks he speaks impudently of yourself, since—before
yourself too; insomuch that I can no longer suffer his
scurrilous abusiveness to you, no more than his love to me.

(*Offers to go.*)

269. last] *Q1;* least *Q2–5, O.*

260.1 *carelessly*] unconcernedly.

SPARKISH.

Nay, nay, madam, pray stay—his love to you! Lord,
madam, has he not spoke yet plain enough?   280

ALITHEA.

Yes, indeed, I should think so.

SPARKISH.

Well then, by the world, a man can't speak civilly to a
woman now but presently she says he makes love to her.
Nay, madam, you shall stay, with your pardon, since you
have not yet understood him, till he has made an *éclaircisse-* 285
ment of his love to you, that is, what kind of love it is.
—[*To* Harcourt.]   Answer to thy catechism. Friend, do you
love my mistress here?

HARCOURT.

Yes, I wish she would not doubt it.

SPARKISH.

But how do you love her?   290

HARCOURT.

With all my soul.

ALITHEA.

I thank him; methinks he speaks plain enough now.

SPARKISH (*to* Alithea).

You are out still. —But with what kind of love, Harcourt?

HARCOURT.

With the best and truest love in the world.

SPARKISH.

Look you there then, that is with no matrimonial love, I'm   295
sure.

ALITHEA.

How's that? Do you say matrimonial love is not best?

SPARKISH.

Gad, I went too far ere I was aware. But speak for thyself,
Harcourt; you said you would not wrong me nor her.

HARCOURT.

No, no, madam, e'en take him for heaven's sake—   300

SPARKISH.

Look you there, madam.

---

283. *presently*] immediately.
285–286. *éclaircissement*] elucidation.

HARCOURT.

Who should in all justice be yours, he that loves you most.

(*Claps his hand on his breast.*)

ALITHEA.

Look you there, Mr. Sparkish, who's that?

SPARKISH.

Who should it be? —Go on, Harcourt.

HARCOURT.

Who loves you more than women titles, or fortune fools.   305

(*Points at* Sparkish.)

SPARKISH.

Look you there, he means me still, for he points at me.

ALITHEA.

Ridiculous!

HARCOURT.

Who can only match your faith and constancy in love.

SPARKISH.

Ay.

HARCOURT.

Who knows, if it be possible, how to value so much beauty 310
and virtue.

SPARKISH.

Ay.

HARCOURT.

Whose love can no more be equaled in the world than that
heavenly form of yours.

SPARKISH.

No.   315

HARCOURT.

Who could no more suffer a rival than your absence, and
yet could no more suspect your virtue than his own constancy
in his love to you.

SPARKISH.

No.

HARCOURT.

Who, in fine, loves you better than his eyes, that first made 320
him love you.

313. no more be] *Q1–4, O;* be no
more *Q5.*

SPARKISH.

Ay—nay, madam, faith, you shan't go till—

ALITHEA.

Have a care, lest you make me stay too long—

SPARKISH.

But till he has saluted you; that I may be assured you are
friends, after his honest advice and declaration. Come, pray, 325
madam, be friends with him.

Enter Mr. Pinchwife, Mrs. Pinchwife.

ALITHEA.

You must pardon me, sir, that I am not yet so obedient to
you.

PINCHWIFE.

What, invite your wife to kiss men? Monstrous! Are you not
ashamed? I will never forgive you.   330

SPARKISH.

Are you not ashamed that I should have more confidence in
the chastity of your family than you have? You must not
teach me; I am a man of honor, sir, though I am frank and
free; I am frank, sir—

PINCHWIFE.

Very frank, sir, to share your wife with your friends.   335

SPARKISH.

He is an humble, menial friend, such as reconciles the
differences of the marriage bed. You know man and wife
do not always agree; I design him for that use, therefore
would have him well with my wife.

PINCHWIFE.

A menial friend! —you will get a great many menial 340
friends by showing your wife as you do.

SPARKISH.

What then? It may be I have a pleasure in't, as I have to
show fine clothes at a playhouse the first day, and count
money before poor rogues.

PINCHWIFE.

He that shows his wife or money will be in danger of having 345

324. he] *Q 1-4, O;* she *Q 5.*   325. his] *Q 1-4, O;* this *Q 5.*

333. *frank*] generous.   336. *menial*] domestic.

them borrowed sometimes.

SPARKISH.

I love to be envied, and would not marry a wife that I alone
could love; loving alone is as dull as eating alone. Is it not a
frank age? and I am a frank person. And to tell you the
truth, it may be I love to have rivals in a wife, they make 350
her seem to a man still but as a kept mistress; and so good
night, for I must to Whitehall. —Madam, I hope you are
now reconciled to my friend; and so I wish you a good night,
madam, and sleep if you can, for tomorrow you know I must
visit you early with a canonical gentleman. Good night, 355
dear Harcourt.

Exit Sparkish.

HARCOURT.

Madam, I hope you will not refuse my visit tomorrow, if it
should be earlier, with a canonical gentleman, than
Mr. Sparkish's.

PINCHWIFE.

This gentlewoman is yet under my care; therefore you 360
must yet forbear your freedom with her, sir.

(*Coming between* Alithea *and* Harcourt.)

HARCOURT.

Must, sir!—

PINCHWIFE.

Yes, sir, she is my sister.

HARCOURT.

'Tis well she is, sir—for I must be her servant, sir.
—Madam—   365

PINCHWIFE.

Come away, sister; we had been gone, if it had not been for
you, and so avoided these lewd rakehells, who seem to
haunt us.

Enter Horner, Dorilant *to them.*

HORNER.

How now, Pinchwife!

PINCHWIFE.

Your servant.   370

359. Sparkish's] *Q1–2, 4–5, O;*   367. lewd] *Q1–4, O; om. Q5.*
Sparkish *Q3.*

−67−

HORNER.

What! I see a little time in the country makes a man turn
wild and unsociable, and only fit to converse with his
horses, dogs, and his herds.

PINCHWIFE.

I have business, sir, and must mind it; your business is
pleasure; therefore you and I must go different ways.   375

HORNER.

Well, you may go on, but this pretty young gentleman—

(Takes hold of Mrs. Pinchwife.)

HARCOURT.

The lady—

DORILANT.

And the maid—

HORNER.

Shall stay with us, for I suppose their business is the same
with ours, pleasure.   380

PINCHWIFE *(aside).*

'Sdeath, he know her, she carries it so sillily! Yet if he does
not, I should be more silly to discover it first.

ALITHEA.

Pray, let us go, sir.

PINCHWIFE.

Come, come—

HORNER *(to* Mrs. Pinchwife).

Had you not rather stay with us? —Prithee, Pinchwife, 385
who is this pretty young gentleman?

PINCHWIFE.

One to whom I'm a guardian. —*(Aside.)*   I wish I could
keep her out of your hands.

HORNER.

Who is he? I never saw anything so pretty in all my life.

PINCHWIFE.

Pshaw! do not look upon him so much; he's a poor bashful 390
youth, you'll put him out of countenance. —Come away,
brother.

(Offers to take her away.)

373. herds] *Q 1–4, O;* herd *Q 5.*   387. a guardian] *Q 1–4, O;* guard-
386. this] *Q 1–4, O;* that *Q 5.*   ian *Q 5.*

HORNER.

Oh, your brother!

PINCHWIFE.

Yes, my wife's brother. —Come, come, she'll stay supper
for us.   395

HORNER.

I thought so, for he is very like her I saw you at the play with,
whom I told you I was in love with.

MRS. PINCHWIFE (*aside*).

O jeminy! Is this he that was in love with me? I am glad
on't, I vow, for he's a curious fine gentleman, and I love
him already too. —(*To* Mr. Pinchwife.)   Is this he, bud?   400

PINCHWIFE (*to his wife*).

Come away, come away.

HORNER.

Why, what haste are you in? Why won't you let me talk with
him?

PINCHWIFE.

Because you'll debauch him; he's yet young and innocent,
and I would not have him debauched for anything in the   405
world. —(*Aside*.)   How she gazes on him! the devil!

HORNER.

Harcourt, Dorilant, look you here; this is the likeness of that·
dowdy he told us of, his wife. Did you ever see a lovelier
creature? The rogue has reason to be jealous of his wife, since
she is like him, for she would make all that see her in love   410
with her.

HARCOURT.

And as I remember now, she is as like him here as can be.

DORILANT.

She is indeed very pretty, if she be like him.

HORNER.

Very pretty? A very pretty commendation! —She is a
glorious creature, beautiful beyond all things I ever beheld.   415

PINCHWIFE.

So, so.

HARCOURT.

More beautiful than a poet's first mistress of imagination.

398. this] *Q1;* that *Q2–5, O.*

HORNER.

Or another man's last mistress of flesh and blood.

MRS. PINCHWIFE.

Nay, now you jeer, sir; pray don't jeer me.

PINCHWIFE.

Come, come. —(*Aside*.) By heavens, she'll discover 420
herself!

HORNER.

I speak of your sister, sir.

PINCHWIFE.

Ay, but saying she was handsome, if like him, made him
blush. —(*Aside*.)   I am upon a rack!

HORNER.

Methinks he is so handsome he should not be a man.   425

PINCHWIFE [*aside*].

Oh, there 'tis out! He has discovered her! I am not able
to suffer any longer. —(*To his wife*.)   Come, come away,
I say.

HORNER.

Nay, by your leave, sir, he shall not go yet. —(*To them*.)
Harcourt, Dorilant, let us torment this jealous rogue a little. 430

HARCOURT. DORILANT.

How?

HORNER.

I'll show you.

PINCHWIFE.

Come, pray let him go, I cannot stay fooling any longer; I
tell you his sister stays supper for us.

HORNER.

Does she? Come then, we'll all go sup with her and thee.   435

PINCHWIFE.

No, now I think on't, having stayed so long for us, I warrant
she's gone to bed. —(*Aside*.)   I wish she and I were well
out of their hands. —Come, I must rise early tomorrow,
come.

HORNER.

Well, then, if she be gone to bed, I wish her and you a good 440
night. But pray, young gentlemen, present my humble
service to her.

MRS. PINCHWIFE.

Thank you heartily, sir.

PINCHWIFE (*aside*).

'Sdeath! she will discover herself yet in spite of me. —He is
something more civil to you, for your kindness to his sister, 445
than I am, it seems.

HORNER.

Tell her, dear sweet little gentleman, for all your brother
there, that you have revived the love I had for her at first
sight in the playhouse.

MRS. PINCHWIFE.

But did you love her indeed, and indeed?   450

PINCHWIFE (*aside*).

So, so. —Away, I say.

HORNER.

Nay, stay. Yes, indeed, and indeed, pray do you tell her so,
and give her this kiss from me.

(*Kisses her.*)

PINCHWIFE (*aside*).

O heavens! what do I suffer! Now 'tis too plain he knows
her, and yet—   455

HORNER.

And this, and this—

(*Kisses her again.*)

MRS. PINCHWIFE.

What do you kiss me for? I am no woman.

PINCHWIFE (*aside*).

So—there, 'tis out. —Come, I cannot, nor will stay any
longer.

HORNER.

Nay, they shall send your lady a kiss too. Here, Harcourt, 460
Dorilant, will you not?   (*They kiss her.*)

PINCHWIFE (*aside*).

How! do I suffer this? Was I not accusing another just now
for this rascally patience, in permitting his wife to be kissed
before his face? Ten thousand ulcers gnaw away their lips!
—Come, come.   465

448. first] *Q1-2, 4-5, O;* the first   463. this] *Q1, 4-5, O;* his *Q2-3.*
Q3.

HORNER.

Good night, dear little gentleman; madam, good night;
farewell, Pinchwife. —(*Apart to* Harcourt *and* Dorilant.)
Did not I tell you I would raise his jealous gall?

Exeunt Horner, Harcourt, *and* Dorilant.

PINCHWIFE.

So, they are gone at last; stay, let me see first if the coach be
at this door.   *Exit.* 470

Horner, Harcourt, Dorilant *return.*

HORNER.

What, not gone yet? Will you be sure to do as I desired you,
sweet sir?

MRS. PINCHWIFE.

Sweet sir, but what will you give me then?

HORNER.

Anything. Come away into the next walk.

Exit Horner, *haling away* Mrs. Pinchwife.

ALITHEA.

Hold, hold! What d'ye do?   475

LUCY.

Stay, stay, hold—

HARCOURT.

Hold, madam, hold! let him present him, he'll come
presently; nay, I will never let you go till you answer my
question.

LUCY.

For God's sake, sir, I must follow 'em.   480

DORILANT.

No, I have something to present you with too; you shan't
follow them.

(Alithea, Lucy *struggling with* Harcourt *and* Dorilant.)

Pinchwife *returns.*

PINCHWIFE.

Where?—how?—what's become of—gone!—whither?

LUCY.

He's only gone with the gentleman, who will give him

484. gentleman] *Q 1–3;* gentlemen
Q 4–5, O.

something, an't please your worship.   485
PINCHWIFE.

Something!—give him something, with a pox!—where are
they?

ALITHEA.

In the next walk only, brother.

PINCHWIFE.

Only, only! Where, where?

Exit Pinchwife, *and returns presently, then goes out again.*

HARCOURT.

What's the matter with him? Why so much concerned? 490
But dearest madam—

ALITHEA.

Pray let me go, sir; I have said and suffered enough already.

HARCOURT.

Then you will not look upon, nor pity, my sufferings?

ALITHEA.

To look upon 'em, when I cannot help 'em, were cruelty,
not pity; therefore I will never see you more.   495

HARCOURT.

Let me then, madam, have my privilege of a banished lover,
complaining or railing, and giving you but a farewell
reason why, if you cannot condescend to marry me, you
should not take that wretch, my rival.

ALITHEA.

He only, not you, since my honor is engaged so far to him, 500
can give me a reason why I should not marry him; but if he
be true, and what I think him to me, I must be so to him.
Your servant, sir.

HARCOURT.

Have women only constancy when 'tis a vice, and, like
fortune, only true to fools?   505

DORILANT (*to* Lucy, *who struggles to get from him*).

Thou shalt not stir, thou robust creature; you see I can deal
with you, therefore you should stay the rather, and be kind.

Enter Pinchwife.

PINCHWIFE.

Gone, gone, not to be found! quite gone! Ten thousand

504. like] *Q 1–3;* are, like *Q 4–5, O.*

---

plagues go with 'em! Which way went they?

ALITHEA.

But into t'other walk, brother.   510

LUCY.

Their business will be done presently sure, an't please your
worship; it can't be long in doing, I'm sure on't.

ALITHEA.

Are they not there?

PINCHWIFE.

No; you know where they are, you infamous wretch,
eternal shame of your family, which you do not dishonor 515
enough yourself, you think, but you must help her to do it
too, thou legion of bawds!

ALITHEA.

Good brother—

PINCHWIFE.

Damned, damned sister!

ALITHEA.

Look you here, she's coming.   520

Enter Mrs. Pinchwife *in man's clothes, running, with her hat under her
arm, full of oranges and dried fruit;* Horner *following.*

MRS. PINCHWIFE.

O dear bud, look you here what I have got, see!

PINCHWIFE (*aside, rubbing his forehead*).

And what I have got here too, which you can't see.

MRS. PINCHWIFE.

The fine gentleman has given me better things yet.

PINCHWIFE.

Has he so? —(*Aside.*)   Out of breath and colored! I must
hold yet.   525

HORNER.

I have only given your little brother an orange, sir.

PINCHWIFE (*to* Horner).

Thank you, sir. —(*Aside.*)   You have only squeezed my
orange, I suppose, and given it me again; yet I must have
a city patience. —(*To his wife.*)   Come, come away.

522. I have] *Q 1–4, O;* have I *Q 5.*

529. *city patience*] patience of city husband cuckolded by aristocrat.

MRS. PINCHWIFE.

Stay, till I have put up my fine things, bud.   530

Enter Sir Jasper Fidget.

SIR JASPER FIDGET.

O Master Horner, come, come, the ladies stay for you;
your mistress, my wife, wonders you make not more haste
to her.

HORNER.

I have stayed this half hour for you here, and 'tis your fault
I am not now with your wife.   535

SIR JASPER FIDGET.

But pray, don't let her know so much; the truth on't is,
I was advancing a certain project to his Majesty about—
I'll tell you.

HORNER.

No, let's go, and hear it at your house. —Good night, sweet
little gentleman. One kiss more; you'll remember me now, 540
I hope.   (*Kisses her.*)

DORILANT.

What, Sir Jasper, will you separate friends? He promised
to sup with us; and if you take him to your house, you'll be
in danger of our company too.

SIR JASPER FIDGET.

Alas, gentlemen, my house is not fit for you; there are none 545
but civil women there, which are not for your turn. He,
you know, can bear with the society of civil women now,
ha, ha, ha! Besides, he's one of my family—he's—he, he, he!

DORILANT.

What is he?

SIR JASPER FIDGET.

Faith, my eunuch, since you'll have it, he, he, he!   550

Exeunt Sir Jasper Fidget, *and* Horner.

DORILANT.

I rather wish thou wert his, or my cuckold. Harcourt, what
a good cuckold is lost there for want of a man to make him
one! Thee and I cannot have Horner's privilege, who can
make use of it.

550.1 *Exeunt*] *Exit Q 1–5, O.*

HARCOURT.

Ay, to poor Horner 'tis like coming to an estate at threescore,   555
when a man can't be the better for't.

PINCHWIFE.

Come.

MRS. PINCHWIFE.

Presently, bud.

DORILANT.

Come, let us go too. —(*To* Alithea.)   Madam, your
servant. —(*To* Lucy.)   Good night, strapper.   560

HARCOURT.

Madam, though you will not let me have a good day or
night, I wish you one; but dare not name the other half of
my wish.

ALITHEA.

Good night, sir, forever.

MRS. PINCHWIFE.

I don't know where to put this here, dear bud, you shall 565
eat it; nay, you shall have part of the fine gentleman's good
things, or treat as you call it, when we come home.

PINCHWIFE.

Indeed, I deserve it, since I furnished the best part of it.

(*Strikes away the orange.*)

The gallant treats, presents, and gives the ball;
But 'tis the absent cuckold pays for all.   570

[*Exeunt.*]

[IV.i]   *In* Pinchwife's *house in the morning.*
                       Lucy, Alithea *dressed in new clothes.*

LUCY.

Well—madam, now have I dressed you, and set you out with
so many ornaments, and spent upon you ounces of essence
and pulvilio; and all this for no other purpose but as people
adorn and perfume a corpse for a stinking secondhand
grave; such or as bad I think Master Sparkish's bed.   5

ALITHEA.

Hold your peace.

---

3. *pulvilio*] a sweet-scented powder.

LUCY.

Nay, madam, I will ask you the reason why you would banish
poor Master Harcourt forever from your sight. How could
you be so hardhearted?

ALITHEA.

'Twas because I was not hardhearted.   10

LUCY.

No, no; 'twas stark love and kindness, I warrant.

ALITHEA.

It was so; I would see him no more because I love him.

LUCY.

Hey-day, a very pretty reason!

ALITHEA.

You do not understand me.

LUCY.

I wish you may yourself.   15

ALITHEA.

I was engaged to marry, you see, another man, whom my
justice will not suffer me to deceive or injure.

LUCY.

Can there be a greater cheat or wrong done to a man than to
give him your person without your heart? I should make a
conscience of it.   20

ALITHEA.

I'll retrieve it for him after I am married a while.

LUCY.

The woman that marries to love better will be as much
mistaken as the wencher that marries to live better. No,
madam, marrying to increase love is like gaming to become
rich; alas, you only lose what little stock you had before.   25

ALITHEA.

I find by your rhetoric you have been bribed to betray me.

LUCY.

Only by his merit, that has bribed your heart, you see,
against your word and rigid honor. But what a devil is this
honor! 'Tis sure a disease in the head, like the megrim, or
falling sickness, that always hurries people away to do   30

---

29. *megrim*] migraine.
30. *falling sickness*] epilepsy.

themselves mischief. Men lose their lives by it; women what's dearer to 'em, their love, the life of life.

ALITHEA.

Come, pray talk you no more of honor, nor Master Harcourt. I wish the other would come to secure my fidelity to him, and his right in me.   35

LUCY.

You will marry him then?

ALITHEA.

Certainly; I have given him already my word, and will my hand too, to make it good when he comes.

LUCY.

Well, I wish I may never stick pin more if he be not an arrant natural to t'other fine gentleman.   40

ALITHEA.

I own he wants the wit of Harcourt, which I will dispense withal for another want he has, which is want of jealousy, which men of wit seldom want.

LUCY.

Lord, madam, what should you do with a fool to your husband? You intend to be honest, don't you? Then that   45
husbandly virtue, credulity, is thrown away upon you.

ALITHEA.

He only that could suspect my virtue should have cause to do it; 'tis Sparkish's confidence in my truth that obliges me to be so faithful to him.

LUCY.

You are not sure his opinion may last.   50

ALITHEA.

I am satisfied 'tis impossible for him to be jealous after the proofs I have had of him. Jealousy in a husband—Heaven defend me from it! It begets a thousand plagues to a poor woman, the loss of her honor, her quiet, and her—

LUCY.

And her pleasure.   55

ALITHEA.

What d'ye mean, impertinent?

---

40. *natural*] simpleton.

LUCY.

Liberty is a great pleasure, madam.

ALITHEA.

I say, loss of her honor, her quiet, nay, her life sometimes;
and what's as bad almost, the loss of this town; that is, she
is sent into the country, which is the last ill usage of a   60
husband to a wife, I think.

LUCY (*aside*).

Oh, does the wind lie there? —Then, of necessity, madam,
you think a man must carry his wife into the country, if he
be wise. The country is as terrible, I find, to our young
English ladies as a monastery to those abroad; and on my   65
virginity, I think they would rather marry a London jailer
than a high sheriff of a county, since neither can stir from
his employment. Formerly women of wit married fools for a
great estate, a fine seat, or the like; but now 'tis for a pretty
seat only in Lincoln's Inn Fields, St. James's Fields, or the 70
Pall Mall.

Enter to them Sparkish, *and* Harcourt *dressed like a parson.*

SPARKISH.

Madam, your humble servant, a happy day to you, and to
us all.

HARCOURT.

Amen.

ALITHEA.

Who have we here?   75

SPARKISH.

My chaplain, faith. O madam, poor Harcourt remembers
his humble service to you; and in obedience to your last
commands, refrains coming into your sight.

ALITHEA.

Is not that he?

SPARKISH.

No, fie, no; but to show that he ne'er intended to hinder our 80
match, has sent his brother here to join our hands. When I
get me a wife, I must get her a chaplain, according to the
custom; this is his brother, and my chaplain.

70–71. *Lincoln's Inn Fields; St. James's Fields; Pall Mall*] fashionable walks.

ALITHEA.

His brother?

LUCY (*aside*).

And your chaplain, to preach in your pulpit then.   85

ALITHEA.

His brother!

SPARKISH.

Nay, I knew you would not believe it. —I told you, sir, she would take you for your brother Frank.

ALITHEA.

Believe it!

LUCY (*aside*).

His brother! ha, ha, he! He has a trick left still, it seems.   90

SPARKISH.

Come, my dearest, pray let us go to church before the canonical hour is past.

ALITHEA.

For shame, you are abused still.

SPARKISH.

By the world, 'tis strange now you are so incredulous.

ALITHEA.

'Tis strange you are so credulous.   95

SPARKISH.

Dearest of my life, hear me. I tell you this is Ned Harcourt of Cambridge, by the world; you see he has a sneaking college look. 'Tis true he's something like his brother Frank, and they differ from each other no more than in their age, for they were twins.   100

LUCY.

Ha, ha, he!

ALITHEA.

Your servant, sir; I cannot be so deceived, though you are. But come, let's hear, how do you know what you affirm so confidently?

SPARKISH.

Why, I'll tell you all. Frank Harcourt coming to me this 105

---

85. (*aside*)] *Q 1–4, O; om. Q 5.*

92. *canonical hour*] between eight A.M. and noon when a marriage ceremony might be performed.

morning, to wish me joy and present his service to you, I
asked him if he could help me to a parson; whereupon he
told me he had a brother in town who was in orders, and he
went straight away and sent him you see there to me.

ALITHEA.

Yes, Frank goes and puts on a black coat, then tells you he 110
is Ned; that's all you have for't.

SPARKISH.

Pshaw, pshaw! I tell you by the same token, the midwife
put her garter about Frank's neck to know 'em asunder, they
were so like.

ALITHEA.

Frank tells you this too.   115

SPARKISH.

Ay, and Ned there too; nay, they are both in a story.

ALITHEA.

So, so; very foolish!

SPARKISH.

Lord, if you won't believe one, you had best try him by your
chambermaid there; for chambermaids must needs know
chaplains from other men, they are so used to 'em.   120

LUCY.

Let's see; nay, I'll be sworn he has the canonical smirk,
and the filthy, clammy palm of a chaplain.

ALITHEA.

Well, most reverend doctor, pray let us make an end of this
fooling.

HARCOURT.

With all my soul, divine, heavenly creature, when you 125
please.

ALITHEA.

He speaks like a chaplain indeed.

SPARKISH.

Why, was there not "soul," "divine," "heavenly," in what
he said?

ALITHEA.

Once more, most impertinent black coat, cease your 130

120. used] *Q 1–4, O;* used so *Q 5.*

-81-

persecution, and let us have a conclusion of this ridiculous love.

HARCOURT (*aside*).

I had forgot; I must suit my style to my coat, or I wear it in vain.

ALITHEA.

I have no more patience left; let us make once an end of 135 this troublesome love, I say.

HARCOURT.

So be it, seraphic lady, when your honor shall think it meet and convenient so to do.

SPARKISH.

Gad, I'm sure none but a chaplain could speak so, I think.

ALITHEA.

Let me tell you, sir, this dull trick will not serve your turn; 140 though you delay our marriage, you shall not hinder it.

HARCOURT.

Far be it from me, munificent patroness, to delay your marriage. I desire nothing more than to marry you presently, which I might do, if you yourself would; for my noble, good-natured, and thrice generous patron here would not 145 hinder it.

SPARKISH.

No, poor man, not I, faith.

HARCOURT.

And now, madam, let me tell you plainly, nobody else shall marry you; by heavens, I'll die first, for I'm sure I should die after it.   150

LUCY [*aside*].

How his love has made him forget his function, as I have seen it in real parsons!

ALITHEA.

That was spoken like a chaplain too! Now you understand him, I hope.

SPARKISH.

Poor man, he takes it heinously to be refused; I can't blame 155 him, 'tis putting an indignity upon him not to be suffered. But you'll pardon me, madam, it shan't be, he shall marry us; come away, pray, madam.

LUCY.

Ha, ha, he! More ado! 'Tis late.

ALITHEA.

Invincible stupidity! I tell you he would marry me as your 160
rival, not as your chaplain.

SPARKISH.

Come, come, madam.   (*Pulling her away.*)

LUCY.

I pray, madam, do not refuse this reverend divine the
honor and satisfaction of marrying you; for I dare say he
has set his heart upon't, good doctor.   165

ALITHEA.

What can you hope, or design by this?

HARCOURT [*aside*].

I could answer her, a reprieve for a day only often revokes
a hasty doom; at worst, if she will not take mercy on me and
let me marry her, I have at least the lover's second pleasure,
hindering my rival's enjoyment, though but for a time.   170

SPARKISH.

Come, madam, 'tis e'en twelve o'clock, and my mother
charged me never to be married out of the canonical hours.
Come, come; Lord, here's such a deal of modesty, I warrant,
the first day.

LUCY.

Yes, an't please your worship, married women show all 175
their modesty the first day, because married men show all
their love the first day.

                    Exeunt Sparkish, Alithea, Harcourt, *and* Lucy.

[IV.ii] *The scene changes to a bedchamber, where appear* Pinchwife,
Mrs. Pinchwife.

PINCHWIFE.

Come, tell me, I say.

MRS. PINCHWIFE.

Lord! han't I told it an hundred times over?

175. an't] *Q 1–4, O;* and *Q 5.*   0.1. Pinchwife] *Q 1–3;* Pinchwife
[IV.ii]   and *Q 4–5, O.*
                                            2. an] *Q 1–4, O;* a *Q 5.*

PINCHWIFE (*aside*).

I would try if, in the repetition of the ungrateful tale, I
could find her altering it in the least circumstance; for if
her story be false, she is so too. —Come, how was't, baggage?   5

MRS. PINCHWIFE.

Lord, what pleasure you take to hear it, sure!

PINCHWIFE.

No, you take more in telling it, I find; but speak, how was't?

MRS. PINCHWIFE.

He carried me up into the house next to the Exchange.

PINCHWIFE.

So; and you two were only in the room.

MRS. PINCHWIFE.

Yes, for he sent away a youth that was there, for some dried   10
fruit and China oranges.

PINCHWIFE.

Did he so? Damn him for it—and for—

MRS. PINCHWIFE.

But presently came up the gentlewoman of the house.

PINCHWIFE.

Oh, 'twas well she did; but what did he do whilst the fruit
came?   15

MRS. PINCHWIFE.

He kissed me an hundred times, and told me he fancied he
kissed my fine sister, meaning me, you know, whom he said
he loved with all his soul, and bid me be sure to tell her so,
and to desire her to be at her window by eleven of the clock
this morning, and he would walk under it at that time.   20

PINCHWIFE (*aside*).

And he was as good as his word, very punctual; a pox
reward him for't.

MRS. PINCHWIFE.

Well, and he said if you were not within, he would come up
to her, meaning me, you know, bud, still.

PINCHWIFE (*aside*).

So—he knew her certainly; but for this confession, I am   25
obliged to her simplicity. —But what, you stood very still

8. the house] *Q1-4, O;* a house   16. an] *Q1-5;* a *O.*
Q5:

when he kissed you?

MRS. PINCHWIFE.

Yes, I warrant you; would you have had me discovered
myself?

PINCHWIFE.

But you told me he did some beastliness to you, as you   30
called it; what was't?

MRS. PINCHWIFE.

Why, he put—

PINCHWIFE.

What?

MRS. PINCHWIFE.

Why, he put the tip of his tongue between my lips, and so
mousled me—and I'said, I'd bite it.   35

PINCHWIFE.

An eternal canker seize it, for a dog!

MRS. PINCHWIFE.

Nay, you need not be so angry with him neither, for to say
truth, he has the sweetest breath I ever knew.

PINCHWIFE.

The devil! —you were satisfied with it then, and would do
it again.   40

MRS. PINCHWIFE.

Not unless he should force me.

PINCHWIFE.

Force you, changeling! I tell you no woman can be forced.

MRS. PINCHWIFE.

Yes, but she may sure by such a one as he, for he's a proper,
goodly strong man; 'tis hard, let me tell you, to resist him.

PINCHWIFE [*aside*].

So, 'tis plain she loves him, yet she has not love enough to   45
make her conceal it from me; but the sight of him will
increase her aversion for me and love for him, and that love
instruct her how to deceive me and satisfy him, all idiot as
she is. Love! 'Twas he gave women first their craft, their
art of deluding; out of nature's hands they came plain, open,   50

28. would you] *Q 1–4, O;* you   31. called] *Q 1–5;* call *O.*
would *Q 5.*

35. *mousled*] rumpled.

silly, and fit for slaves, as she and Heaven intended 'em;
but damned love—well—I must strangle that little monster
whilst I can deal with him. —Go fetch pen, ink, and paper
out of the next room.

MRS. PINCHWIFE.

Yes, bud.   *Exit* Mrs. Pinchwife.   55

PINCHWIFE (*aside*).

Why should women have more invention in love than men?
It can only be because they have more desires, more soliciting
passions, more lust, and more of the devil.

Mrs. Pinchwife *returns.*

Come, minx, sit down and write.

MRS. PINCHWIFE.

Ay, dear bud, but I can't do't very well.   60

PINCHWIFE.

I wish you could not at all.

MRS. PINCHWIFE.

But what should I write for?

PINCHWIFE.

I'll have you write a letter to your lover.

MRS. PINCHWIFE.

O Lord, to the fine gentleman a letter!

PINCHWIFE.

Yes, to the fine gentleman.   65

MRS. PINCHWIFE.

Lord, you do but jeer; sure you jest.

PINCHWIFE.

I am not so merry; come, write as I bid you.

MRS. PINCHWIFE.

What, do you think I am a fool?

PINCHWIFE [*aside*].

She's afraid I would not dictate any love to him, therefore
she's unwilling. —But you had best begin.   70

MRS. PINCHWIFE.

Indeed, and indeed, but I won't, so I won't!

PINCHWIFE.

Why?

---

56. (*aside*)] *Q 1–4, O; om. Q 5.*

MRS. PINCHWIFE.

Because he's in town; you may send for him if you will.

PINCHWIFE.

Very well, you would have him brought to you; is it come
to this? I say, take the pen and write, or you'll provoke me.   75

MRS. PINCHWIFE.

Lord, what d'ye make a fool of me for? Don't I know that
letters are never writ but from the country to London, and
from London into the country? Now he's in town, and I
am in town too; therefore I can't write to him, you know.

PINCHWIFE (*aside*).

So, I am glad it is no worse; she is innocent enough yet.   80
—Yes, you may, when your husband bids you, write letters
to people that are in town.

MRS. PINCHWIFE.

Oh, may I so? Then I'm satisfied.

PINCHWIFE.

Come, begin. —(*Dictates.*)   "Sir"—

MRS. PINCHWIFE.

Shan't I say, "Dear Sir"? You know one says always   85
something more than bare "Sir."

PINCHWIFE.

Write as I bid you, or I will write "whore" with this penknife
in your face.

MRS. PINCHWIFE.

Nay, good bud—(*She writes.*)   "Sir"—

PINCHWIFE.

"Though I suffered last night your nauseous, loathed kisses   90
and embraces"—Write.

MRS. PINCHWIFE.

Nay, why should I say so? You know I told you he had a
sweet breath.

PINCHWIFE.

Write!

MRS. PINCHWIFE.

Let me but put out "loathed."   95

PINCHWIFE.

Write, I say!

81. Yes] *Q 1–2, 4–5, O;* yet *Q 3.*

MRS. PINCHWIFE.

Well then. (*Writes.*)

PINCHWIFE.

Let's see, what have you writ? —(*Takes the paper, and reads.*)
"Though I suffered last night your kisses and embraces"—
Thou impudent creature! Where is "nauseous" and 100
"loathed"?

MRS. PINCHWIFE.

I can't abide to write such filthy words.

PINCHWIFE.

Once more write as I'd have you, and question it not, or I
will spoil thy writing with this. (*Holds up the penknife.*)
I will stab out those eyes that cause my mischief. 105

MRS. PINCHWIFE.

O Lord, I will!

PINCHWIFE.

So—so—let's see now! —(*Reads.*) "Though I suffered last
night your nauseous, loathed kisses and embraces"—go on—
"yet I would not have you presume that you shall ever repeat
them." —So. 110

(*She writes.*)

MRS. PINCHWIFE.

I have writ it.

PINCHWIFE.

On then. —"I then concealed myself from your knowledge,
to avoid your insolencies"—

(*She writes.*)

MRS. PINCHWIFE.

So—

PINCHWIFE.

"The same reason, now I am out of your hands"— 115

(*She writes.*)

MRS. PINCHWIFE.

So—

PINCHWIFE.

"Makes me own to you my unfortunate, though innocent
frolic, of being in man's clothes"—

(*She writes.*)

MRS. PINCHWIFE.

So—

PINCHWIFE.

"That you may forevermore cease to pursue her, who hates 120
and detests you"—

(She writes on.)

MRS. PINCHWIFE.

So-h—   *(Sighs.)*

PINCHWIFE.

What, do you sigh? —"detests you—as much as she loves
her husband and her honor."

MRS. PINCHWIFE.

I vow, husband, he'll ne'er believe I should write such a 125
letter.

PINCHWIFE.

What, he'd expect a kinder from you? Come, now your
name only.

MRS. PINCHWIFE.

What, shan't I say, "Your most faithful, humble servant
till death"?   130

PINCHWIFE.

No, tormenting fiend! —*(Aside.)* Her style, I find, would
be very soft. —Come, wrap it up now, whilst I go fetch wax
and a candle; and write on the backside, "For Mr. Horner."

Exit Pinchwife.

MRS. PINCHWIFE.

"For Mr. Horner."—So, I am glad he has told me his name.
Dear Mr. Horner! But why should I send thee such a letter 135
that will vex thee, and make thee angry with me? —Well,
I will not send it—Ay, but then my husband will kill me—
for I see plainly he won't let me love Mr. Horner—but what
care I for my husband? —I won't, so I won't send poor
ı⁄r. Horner such a letter—But then my husband—But oh, 140
what if I writ at bottom, my husband made me write it?
—Ay, but then my husband would see't—Can one have no
shift? Ah, a London woman would have had a hundred
presently. Stay—what if I should write a letter, and wrap
it up like this, and write upon't too? Ay, but then my 145
husband would see't—I don't know what to do—But yet

131. fiend] *Q1, O;* friend *Q2–5.*   142. would] *Q1–4, O;* will *Q5.*

y'vads I'll try, so I will—for I will not send this letter to
poor Mr. Horner, come what will on't.

(She writes, and repeats what she hath writ.)

"Dear, sweet Mr. Horner"—so—"my husband would
have me send you a base, rude, unmannerly letter—but I   150
won't"—so—"and would have me forbid you loving me—
but I won't"—so—"and would have me say to you, I hate
you, poor Mr. Horner—but I won't tell a lie for him"—there
—"for I'm sure if you and I were in the country at cards
together"—so—"I could not help treading on your toe   155
under the table"—so—"or rubbing knees with you, and
staring in your face till you saw me"—very well—"and
then looking down, and blushing for an hour together"—
so—"but I must make haste before my husband comes; and
now he has taught me to write letters, you shall have longer   160
ones from me, who am, dear, dear, poor, dear Mr. Horner,
your most humble friend, and servant to command till
death, Margery Pinchwife."

Stay, I must give him a hint at bottom—so—now wrap
it up just like t'other—so—now write, "For Mr. Horner"—   165
But, oh now, what shall I do with it? for here comes my
husband.

Enter Pinchwife.

PINCHWIFE *(aside)*.

I have been detained by a sparkish coxcomb, who pretended
a visit to me; but I fear 'twas to my wife. —What, have you
done?   170

MRS. PINCHWIFE.

Ay, ay, bud, just now.

PINCHWIFE.

Let's see't; what d'ye tremble for? What, you would not
have it go?

MRS. PINCHWIFE.

Here. —*(Aside.)*   No, I must not give him that; so I had
been served if I had given him this.   175

---

159. comes] *Q4–5, O;* come *Q1–3.*

147. *y'vads*] in faith.

PINCHWIFE.

(*He opens, and reads the first letter.*)   Come, where's the wax and seal?

MRS. PINCHWIFE (*aside*).

Lord, what shall I do now? Nay, then, I have it. —Pray let me see't. Lord, you think me so arrant a fool I cannot seal a letter; I will do't, so I will.   180

(*Snatches the letter from him, changes it for the other, seals it, and delivers it to him.*)

PINCHWIFE.

Nay, I believe you will learn that, and other things too, which I would not have you.

MRS. PINCHWIFE.

So, han't I done it curiously? —(*Aside.*)   I think I have; there's my letter going to Mr. Horner, since he'll needs have me send letters to folks.   185

PINCHWIFE.

'Tis very well; but I warrant you would not have it go now?

MRS. PINCHWIFE.

Yes, indeed, but I would, bud, now.

PINCHWIFE.

Well, you are a good girl then. Come, let me lock you up in your chamber till I come back; and be sure you come not within three strides of the window when I am gone, for I   190 have a spy in the street.

Exit Mrs. Pinchwife.

(Pinchwife *locks the door.*)   At least, 'tis fit she think so. If we do not cheat women, they'll cheat us; and fraud may be justly used with secret enemies, of which a wife is the most dangerous; and he that has a handsome one to keep, and a   195 frontier town, must provide against treachery rather than open force. Now I have secured all within, I'll deal with the foe without with false intelligence.   (*Holds up the letter.*)

Exit Pinchwife.

191.1. *Exit* Mrs. Pinchwife] *Q1–4,*   192. think] *Q1–5;* thinks *O.*
O; om. Q5.

183. *curiously*] cleverly, neatly.

[IV.iii] *The scene changes to* Horner's *lodging*. Quack *and* Horner.

QUACK.

> Well, sir, how fadges the new design? Have you not the
> luck of all your brother projectors, to deceive only yourself
> at last?

HORNER.

> No, good domine doctor, I deceive you, it seems, and others
> too; for the grave matrons and old, rigid husbands think me   5
> as unfit for love as they are; but their wives, sisters, and
> daughters know some of 'em better things already.

QUACK.

> Already!

HORNER.

> Already, I say. Last night I was drunk with half a dozen of
> your civil persons, as you call 'em, and people of honor, and   10
> so was made free of their society and dressing rooms forever
> hereafter; and am already come to the privileges of sleeping
> upon their pallets, warming smocks, tying shoes and
> garters, and the like, doctor, already, already, doctor.

QUACK.

> You have made use of your time, sir.   15

HORNER.

> I tell thee, I am now no more interruption to 'em when they
> sing, or talk, bawdy than a little squab French page who
> speaks no English.

QUACK.

> But do civil persons and women of honor drink, and sing
> bawdy songs?   20

HORNER.

> Oh, amongst friends, amongst friends. For your bigots in
> honor are just like those in religion; they fear the eye of the
> world more than the eye of Heaven, and think there is no
> virtue but railing at vice, and no sin but giving scandal.
> They rail at a poor, little, kept player, and keep themselves   25
> some young, modest pulpit comedian to be privy to their

---

1. you not] *Q1–4, O;* not you *Q5.*

1. *fadges*] succeeds.   17. *squab*] squat and plump.
26. *pulpit comedian*] chaplain.

sins in their closets, not to tell 'em of them in their chapels.

QUACK.

Nay, the truth on't is, priests amongst the women now have
quite got the better of us lay confessors, physicians.

HORNER.

And they are rather their patients, but—   30

Enter My Lady Fidget, *looking about her.*

Now we talk of women of honor, here comes one. Step
behind the screen there, and but observe if I have not
particular privileges with the women of reputation already,
doctor, already.   [Quack *steps behind screen.*]

LADY FIDGET.

Well, Horner, am not I a woman of honor? You see I'm as   35
good as my word.

HORNER.

And you shall see, madam, I'll not be behindhand with
you in honor; and I'll be as good as my word too, if you
please but to withdraw into the next room.

LADY FIDGET.

But first, my dear sir, you must promise to have a care of   40
my dear honor.

HORNER.

If you talk a word more of your honor, you'll make me
incapable to wrong it. To talk of honor in the mysteries of
love is like talking of Heaven or the Deity in an operation of
witchcraft, just when you are employing the devil; it makes   45
the charm impotent.

LADY FIDGET.

Nay, fie! let us not be smutty. But you talk of mysteries and
bewitching to me; I don't understand you.

HORNER.

I tell you, madam, the word "money" in a mistress's mouth,
at such a nick of time, is not a more disheartening sound to   50
a younger brother than that of "honor" to an eager lover
like myself.

28. amongst] *Q1–2, 4–5, O;* among
Q3.

LADY FIDGET.

But you can't blame a lady of my reputation to be chary.

HORNER.

Chary! I have been chary of it already, by the report I have
caused of myself.   55

LADY FIDGET.

Ay, but if you should ever let other women know that dear
secret, it would come out. Nay, you must have a great care
of your conduct; for my acquaintance are so censorious
(oh, 'tis a wicked, censorious world, Mr. Horner!), I say,
are so censorious and detracting that perhaps they'll talk,   60
to the prejudice of my honor, though you should not let
them know the dear secret.

HORNER.

Nay, madam, rather than they shall prejudice your honor,
I'll prejudice theirs; and to serve you, I'll lie with 'em all,
make the secret their own, and then they'll keep it. I am a   65
Machiavel in love, madam.

LADY FIDGET.

Oh, no, sir, not that way.

HORNER.

Nay, the devil take me if censorious women are to be
silenced any other way.

LADY FIDGET.

A secret is better kept, I hope, by a single person than a   70
multitude; therefore pray do not trust anybody else with it,
dear, dear Mr. Horner.

(Embracing him.)

Enter Sir Jasper Fidget.

SIR JASPER FIDGET.

How now!

LADY FIDGET *(aside)*.

Oh, my husband!—prevented—and what's almost as bad,
found with my arms about another man—that will appear   75
too much—what shall I say?

Sir Jasper, come hither. I am trying if Mr. Horner were

71. pray] *Q 1–4, O; om. Q 5.*   72.1. *(Embracing him.)*] *Q 1–3; om.*
Q 4–5, O.

ticklish, and he's as ticklish as can be; I love to torment the
confounded toad; let you and I tickle him.

SIR JASPER FIDGET.

No, your ladyship will tickle him better without me, I   80
suppose. But is this your buying china? I thought you had
been at the china house.

HORNER (*aside*).

China house! That's my cue, I must take it. —A pox! can't
you keep your impertinent wives at home? Some men are
troubled with the husbands, but I with the wives. But I'd   85
have you to know, since I cannot be your journeyman by
night, I will not be your drudge by day, to squire your wife
about and be your man of straw, or scarecrow, only to pies
and jays, that would be nibbling at your forbidden fruit;
I shall be shortly the hackney gentleman-usher of the town.   90

SIR JASPER FIDGET (*aside*).

He, he, he! Poor fellow, he's in the right on't, faith; to
squire women about for other folks is as ungrateful an
employment as to tell money for other folks. —He, he, he!
Ben't angry, Horner.

LADY FIDGET.

No, 'tis I have more reason to be angry, who am left by you 95
to go abroad indecently alone; or, what is more indecent, to
pin myself upon such ill-bred people of your acquaintance
as this is.

SIR JASPER FIDGET.

Nay, prithee what has he done?

LADY FIDGET.

Nay, he has done nothing.   100

SIR JASPER FIDGET.

But what d'ye take ill, if he has done nothing?

LADY FIDGET.

Ha, ha, ha! Faith, I can't but laugh, however; why, d'ye
think the unmannerly toad would come down to me to the
coach? I was fain to come up to fetch him, or go without

103. would] *Q5;* would not *Q1–4,*
O.

88–89. *pies and jays*] fops.   90. *hackney*] hired.
93. *tell*] count.

him, which I was resolved not to do; for he knows china very   105
well, and has himself very good, but will not let me see it lest
I should beg some. But I will find it out, and have what I
came for yet.

Exit Lady Fidget, *and locks the door, followed by* Horner *to the door.*

HORNER (*apart to* Lady Fidget).

Lock the door, madam. —So, she has got into my chamber,
and locked me out. Oh, the impertinency of womankind! 110
Well, Sir Jasper, plain dealing is a jewel; if ever you suffer
your wife to trouble me again here, she shall carry you home
a pair of horns, by my Lord Mayor she shall; though I
cannot furnish you myself, you are sure, yet I'll find a way.

SIR JASPER FIDGET (*aside*).

Ha, ha, he! At my first coming in and finding her arms about 115
him, tickling him it seems, I was half jealous, but now I see
my folly. —He, he, he! Poor Horner.

HORNER.

Nay, though you laugh now, 'twill be my turn ere long.
Oh, women, more impertinent, more cunning, and more
mischievous than their monkeys, and to me almost as ugly! 120
Now is she throwing my things about and rifling all I have,
but I'll get in to her the back way, and so rifle her for it.

SIR JASPER FIDGET.

Ha, ha, ha! Poor angry Horner.

HORNER.

Stay here a little; I'll ferret her out to you presently, I
warrant.   125

Exit Horner *at t'other door.*

SIR JASPER FIDGET.

Wife! My Lady Fidget! Wife! He is coming in to you the
back way.

(Sir Jasper *calls through the door to his wife; she answers from within.*)

LADY FIDGET.

Let him come, and welcome, which way he will.

SIR JASPER FIDGET.

He'll catch you, and use you roughly, and be too strong for
you.   130

LADY FIDGET.

Don't you trouble yourself, let him if he can.

QUACK (*behind*).

This indeed I could not have believed from him, nor any but my own eyes.

Enter Mrs. Squeamish.

MRS. SQUEAMISH.

Where's this woman-hater, this toad, this ugly, greasy, dirty sloven?   135

SIR JASPER FIDGET [*aside*].

So, the women all will have him ugly; methinks he is a comely person, but his wants make his form contemptible to 'em; and 'tis e'en as my wife said yesterday, talking of him, that a proper handsome eunuch was as ridiculous a thing as a gigantic coward.   140

MRS. SQUEAMISH.

Sir Jasper, your servant. Where is the odious beast?

SIR JASPER FIDGET.

He's within in his chamber, with my wife; she's playing the wag with him.

MRS. SQUEAMISH.

Is she so? And he's a clownish beast, he'll give her no quarter, he'll play the wag with her again, let me tell you. 145 Come, let's go help her. —What, the door's locked?

SIR JASPER FIDGET.

Ay, my wife locked it.

MRS. SQUEAMISH.

Did she so? Let us break it open then.

SIR JASPER FIDGET.

No, no, he'll do her no hurt.

MRS. SQUEAMISH.

No. —(*Aside.*)   But is there no other way to get in to 'em? 150 Whither goes this? I will disturb 'em.

Exit [Mrs.] Squeamish *at another door.*

Enter Old Lady Squeamish.

OLD LADY SQUEAMISH.

Where is this harlotry, this impudent baggage, this rambling tomrig? O Sir Jasper, I'm glad to see you here, did you not

---

153. *tomrig*] tomboy.

see my vile grandchild come in hither just now?

SIR JASPER FIDGET.

Yes.   155

OLD LADY SQUEAMISH.

Ay, but where is she then? where is she? Lord, Sir Jasper,
I have e'en rattled myself to pieces in pursuit of her. But
can you tell what she makes here? They say below, no
woman lodges here.

SIR JASPER FIDGET.

No.   160

OLD LADY SQUEAMISH.

No! What does she here then? Say, if it be not a woman's
lodging, what makes she here? But are you sure no woman
lodges here?

SIR JASPER FIDGET.

No, nor no man neither; this is Mr. Horner's lodging.

OLD LADY SQUEAMISH.

Is it so, are you sure?   165

SIR JASPER FIDGET.

Yes, yes.

OLD LADY SQUEAMISH.

So; then there's no hurt in't, I hope. But where is he?

SIR JASPER FIDGET.

He's in the next room with my wife.

OLD LADY SQUEAMISH.

Nay, if you trust him with your wife, I may with my Biddy.
They say he's a merry harmless man now, e'en as harmless   170
a man as ever came out of Italy with a good voice, and as
pretty harmless company for a lady as a snake without his
teeth.

SIR JASPER FIDGET.

Ay, ay, poor man.

Enter Mrs. Squeamish.

MRS. SQUEAMISH.

I can't find 'em. —Oh, are you here, Grandmother? I   175
followed, you must know, my Lady Fidget hither; 'tis the

154. vile] vild *Q 1–5, O.*   171. and as] *Q 1–5;* and is *O.*

170–171. *as harmless . . . Italy*] castrated singer of period.

prettiest lodging, and I have been staring on the prettiest
pictures.

Enter Lady Fidget *with a piece of china in her hand, and* Horner *following.*

LADY FIDGET.

And I have been toiling and moiling for the prettiest piece of
china, my dear.   180

HORNER.

Nay, she has been too hard for me, do what I could.

MRS. SQUEAMISH.

O Lord, I'll have some china too. Good Mr. Horner, don't
think to give other people china, and me none; come in with
me too.

HORNER.

Upon my honor, I have none left now.   185

MRS. SQUEAMISH.

Nay, nay, I have known you deny your china before now,
but you shan't put me off so. Come.

HORNER.

This lady had the last there.

LADY FIDGET.

Yes, indeed, madam, to my certain knowledge he has no
more left.   190

MRS. SQUEAMISH.

Oh, but it may be he may have some you could not find.

LADY FIDGET.

What, d'ye think if he had had any left, I would not have
had it too? For we women of quality never think we have
china enough.

HORNER.

Do not take it ill, I cannot make china for you all, but I will 195
have a roll-wagon for you too, another time.

MRS. SQUEAMISH.

Thank you, dear toad.

LADY FIDGET (*to* Horner, *aside*).

What do you mean by that promise?

HORNER (*apart to* Lady Fidget).

Alas, she has an innocent, literal understanding.

---

179. *moiling*] laboring.
196 *roll-wagon*] a low-wheeled vehicle for carrying goods.

OLD LADY SQUEAMISH.

Poor Mr. Horner! He has enough to do to please you all, 200
I see.

HORNER.

Ay, madam, you see how they use me.

OLD LADY SQUEAMISH.

Poor gentleman, I pity you.

HORNER.

I thank you, madam. I could never find pity but from such
reverend ladies as you are; the young ones will never spare 205
a man.

MRS. SQUEAMISH.

Come, come, beast, and go dine with us, for we shall want
a man at ombre after dinner.

HORNER.

That's all their use of me, madam, you see.

MRS. SQUEAMISH.

Come, sloven, I'll lead you, to be sure of you.   210
                                        (*Pulls him by the cravat.*)

OLD LADY SQUEAMISH.

Alas, poor man, how she tugs him! Kiss, kiss her; that's the
way to make such nice women quiet.

HORNER.

No, madam, that remedy is worse than the torment; they
know I dare suffer anything rather than do it.

OLD LADY SQUEAMISH.

Prithee kiss her, and I'll give you her picture in little, that 215
you admired so last night; prithee do.

HORNER.

Well, nothing but that could bribe me; I love a woman only
in effigy and good painting, as much as I hate them. I'll do't,
for I could adore the devil well painted.

                                        (*Kisses* Mrs. Squeamish.)

MRS. SQUEAMISH.

Foh, you filthy toad! Nay, now I've done jesting.   220

OLD LADY SQUEAMISH.

Ha, ha, ha! I told you so.

MRS. SQUEAMISH.

Foh! a kiss of his—

SIR JASPER FIDGET.

Has no more hurt in't than one of my spaniel's.

MRS. SQUEAMISH.

Nor no more good neither.

QUACK (*behind*).

I will now believe anything he tells me.   225

Enter Mr. Pinchwife.

LADY FIDGET.

O Lord, here's a man! Sir Jasper, my mask, my mask!
I would not be seen here for the world.

SIR JASPER FIDGET.

What, not when I am with you?

LADY FIDGET.

No, no, my honor—let's be gone.

MRS. SQUEAMISH.

Oh, Grandmother, let us be gone; make haste, make haste, 230
I know not how he may censure us.

LADY FIDGET.

Be found in the lodging of anything like a man! Away!

Exeunt Sir Jasper, Lady Fidget, Old Lady Squeamish, Mrs. Squeamish.

QUACK (*behind*).

What's here? another cuckold? He looks like one, and none
else sure have any business with him.

HORNER.

Well, what brings my dear friend hither?   235

PINCHWIFE.

Your impertinency.

HORNER.

My impertinency! —Why, you gentlemen that have got
handsome wives think you have a privilege of saying anything to your friends, and are as brutish as if you were our
creditors.   240

PINCHWIFE.

No, sir, I'll ne'er trust you any way.

HORNER.

But why not, dear Jack? Why diffide in me thou know'st so
well?

235. Well] *Q 1–4, O; om. Q 5.*   239. our] *Q 1–4, O; om. Q 5.*

242. *diffide in*] distrust.

PINCHWIFE.

Because I do know you so well.

HORNER.

Han't I been always thy friend, honest Jack, always ready 245
to serve thee, in love or battle, before thou wert married, and
am so still?

PINCHWIFE.

I believe so; you would be my second now indeed.

HORNER.

Well then, dear Jack, why so unkind, so grum, so strange to
me? Come, prithee kiss me, dear rogue. Gad, I was always, 250
I say, and am still as much thy servant as—

PINCHWIFE.

As I am yours, sir. What, you would send a kiss to my wife,
is that it?

HORNER.

So, there 'tis—a man can't show his friendship to a married
man, but presently he talks of his wife to you. Prithee, let 255
thy wife alone, and let thee and I be all one, as we were wont.
What, thou art as shy of my kindness as a Lombard Street
alderman of a courtier's civility at Locket's.

PINCHWIFE.

But you are overkind to me, as kind as if I were your cuckold
already; yet I must confess you ought to be kind and civil to 260
me, since I am so kind, so civil to you, as to bring you this.
Look you there, sir.

(Delivers him a letter.)

HORNER.

What is't?

PINCHWIFE.

Only a love letter, sir.

HORNER.

From whom?—how! this is from your wife!—hum—and 265
hum—   *(Reads.)*

PINCHWIFE.

Even from my wife, sir. Am I not wondrous kind and civil

267. I not] *Q1–4, O;* not I *Q5.*

---

257. *Lombard Street*] known for goldsmiths, hence having money.
258. *Locket's*] fashionable restaurant.

to you now too? —(*Aside.*)   But you'll not think her so.

PINCHWIFE (*aside*).

Ha! Is this a trick of his or hers?

PINCHWIFE.

The gentleman's surprised, I find.   What, you expected a   270
kinder letter?

HORNER.

No, faith, not I, how could I?

PINCHWIFE.

Yes, yes, I'm sure you did; a man so well made as you are
must needs be disappointed if the women declare not their
passion at first sight or opportunity.   275

HORNER [*aside*].

But what should this mean? Stay, the postscript. —(*Reads
aside.*)   "Be sure you love me whatsoever my husband says
to the contrary, and let him not see this, lest he should come
home and pinch me, or kill my squirrel." —(*Aside.*)   It
seems he knows not what the letter contains.   280

PINCHWIFE.

Come, ne'er wonder at it so much.

HORNER.

Faith, I can't help it.

PINCHWIFE.

Now, I think, I have deserved your infinite friendship and
kindness, and have showed myself sufficiently an obliging˙
kind friend and husband; am I not so, to bring a letter from   285
my wife to her gallant?

HORNER.

Ay, the devil take me, art thou the most obliging, kind friend
and husband in the world, ha, ha!

PINCHWIFE.

Well, you may be merry, sir; but in short I must tell you, sir,
my honor will suffer no jesting.   290

HORNER.

What dost thou mean?

PINCHWIFE.

Does the letter want a comment? Then know, sir, though I
have been so civil a husband as to bring you a letter from my

285. so] *Q 1–4, O; om. Q 5.*

wife, to let you kiss and court her to my face, I will not be a
cuckold, sir, I will not.   295

HORNER.

Thou art mad with jealousy. I never saw thy wife in my life
but at the play yesterday, and I know not if it were she or no.
I court her, kiss her!

PINCHWIFE.

I will not be a cuckold, I say; there will be danger in making
me a cuckold.   300

HORNER.

Why, wert thou not well cured of thy last clap?

PINCHWIFE.

I wear a sword.

HORNER.

It should be taken from thee lest thou shouldst do thyself a
mischief with it; thou art mad, man.

PINCHWIFE.

As mad as I am, and as merry as you are, I must have more   305
reason from you ere we part. I say again, though you kissed
and courted last night my wife in man's clothes, as she
confesses in her letter—

HORNER (*aside*).

Ha!

PINCHWIFE.

Both she and I say, you must not design it again, for you   310
have mistaken your woman, as you have done your man.

HORNER (*aside*).

Oh—I understand something now. —Was that thy wife?
Why wouldst thou not tell me 'twas she? Faith, my freedom
with her was your fault, not mine.

PINCHWIFE (*aside*).

Faith, so 'twas.   315

HORNER.

Fie! I'd never do't to a woman before her husband's face,
sure.

PINCHWIFE.

But I had rather you should do't to my wife before my face

313. thou not] *Q1–2, 4–5, O;* not
thou *Q3.*

than behind my back, and that you shall never do.

HORNER.

No—you will hinder me.   320

PINCHWIFE.

If I would not hinder you, you see by her letter, she would.

HORNER.

Well, I must e'en acquiesce then, and be contented with
what she writes.

PINCHWIFE.

I'll assure you 'twas voluntarily writ; I had no hand in't,
you may believe me.   325

HORNER.

I do believe thee, faith.

PINCHWIFE.

And believe her too, for she's an innocent creature, has no
dissembling in her; and so fare you well, sir.

HORNER.

Pray, however, present my humble service to her, and tell
her I will obey her letter to a tittle, and fulfill her desires, 330
be what they will, or with what difficulty soever I do't, and
you shall be no more jealous of me, I warrant her and you.

PINCHWIFE.

Well, then, fare you well, and play with any man's honor
but mine, kiss any man's wife but mine, and welcome.

                                    Exit Mr. Pinchwife.

HORNER.

Ha, ha, ha! doctor.   335

QUACK.

It seems he has not heard the report of you, or does not
believe it.

HORNER.

Ha, ha! Now, doctor, what think you?

QUACK.

Pray let's see the letter—hum—(*Reads the letter.*) "for—
dear—love you"—   340

HORNER.

I wonder how she could contrive it! What say'st thou to't?

319. shall] *Q1–4, O;* should *Q5.*

'Tis an original.

QUACK.

So are your cuckolds, too, originals, for they are like no other
common cuckolds, and I will henceforth believe it not
impossible for you to cuckold the Grand Signior amidst his 345
guards of eunuchs, that I say.

HORNER.

And I say for the letter, 'tis the first love letter that ever was
without flames, darts, fates, destinies, lying and dissembling
in't.

Enter Sparkish, *pulling in* Mr. Pinchwife.

SPARKISH.

Come back, you are a pretty brother-in-law, neither go to 350
church, nor to dinner with your sister bride!

PINCHWIFE.

My sister denies her marriage, and you see is gone away
from you dissatisfied.

SPARKISH.

Pshaw! upon a foolish scruple, that our parson was not in
lawful orders, and did not say all the Common Prayer; but 355
'tis her modesty only, I believe. But let women be never so
modest the first day, they'll be sure to come to themselves by
night, and I shall have enough of her then. In the meantime,
Harry Horner, you must dine with me; I keep my wedding
at my aunt's in the Piazza.   360

HORNER.

Thy wedding! What stale maid has lived to despair of a
husband, or what young one of a gallant?

SPARKISH.

Oh, your servant, sir—this gentleman's sister then—no stale
maid.

HORNER.

I'm sorry for't.   365

PINCHWIFE (*aside*).

How comes he so concerned for her?

SPARKISH.

You sorry for't? Why, do you know any ill by her?

---

345. *Grand Signior*] Turkish sultan with his harem.
360. *Piazza*] arcade by Covent Garden.

HORNER.

No, I know none but by thee; 'tis for her sake, not yours,
and another man's sake that might have hoped, I thought.

SPARKISH.

Another man! another man! What is his name?   370

HORNER.

Nay, since 'tis past he shall be nameless. —(*Aside.*)   Poor
Harcourt! I am sorry thou hast missed her.

PINCHWIFE (*aside*).

He seems to be much troubled at the match.

SPARKISH.

Prithee tell me—nay, you shan't go, brother.

PINCHWIFE.

I must of necessity, but I'll come to you to dinner.   375

Exit Pinchwife.

SPARKISH.

But, Harry, what, have I a rival in my wife already? But
with all my heart, for he may be of use to me hereafter; for
though my hunger is now my sauce, and I can fall on heartily
without, but the time will come when a rival will be as good
sauce for a married man to a wife as an orange to veal.   380

HORNER.

O thou damned rogue! Thou hast set my teeth on edge with
thy orange.

SPARKISH.

Then let's to dinner—there I was with you again. Come.

HORNER.

But who dines with thee?

SPARKISH.

My friends and relations, my brother Pinchwife, you see,   385
of your acquaintance.

HORNER.

And his wife?

SPARKISH.

No, gad, he'll ne'er let her come amongst us good fellows.
Your stingy country coxcomb keeps his wife from his friends,
as he does his little firkin of ale for his own drinking, and a 390

375. to dinner] *Q1–4, O;* at *Q5.*

---

390. *firkin*] cask.

gentleman can't get a smack on't; but his servants, when his
back is turned, broach it at their pleasures, and dust it away,
ha, ha, ha! Gad, I am witty, I think, considering I was
married today, by the world; but come—

HORNER.

No, I will not dine with you, unless you can fetch her too. 395

SPARKISH.

Pshaw! what pleasure canst thou have with women now,
Harry?

HORNER.

My eyes are not gone; I love a good prospect yet, and will
not dine with you unless she does too. Go fetch her, therefore, but do not tell her husband 'tis for my sake.   400

SPARKISH.

Well, I'll go try what I can do; in the meantime come away
to my aunt's lodging, 'tis in the way to Pinchwife's.

HORNER.

The poor woman has called for aid, and stretched forth her
hand, doctor; I cannot but help her over the pale out of
the briars.   405

                              Exeunt Sparkish, Horner, Quack.

[IV.iv]   *The scene changes to* Pinchwife's *house.*
Mrs. Pinchwife *alone, leaning on her elbow. A table, pen, ink, and paper.*

MRS. PINCHWIFE.

Well, 'tis e'en so, I have got the London disease they call
love; I am sick of my husband, and for my gallant. I have
heard this distemper called a fever, but methinks 'tis liker
an ague, for when I think of my husband, I tremble and am
in a cold sweat and have inclinations to vomit; but when I   5
think of my gallant, dear Mr. Horner, my hot fit comes and
I am all in a fever, indeed, and as in other fevers my own
chamber is tedious to me, and I would fain be removed to
his, and then methinks I should be well. Ah, poor Mr.
Horner! Well, I cannot, will not stay here; therefore I'll   10
make an end of my letter to him, which shall be a finer

391. smack] *Q 1–4, O;* snack *Q 5.*

391. *smack*] taste.   392. *dust it away*] drink up quickly.

letter than my last, because I have studied it like anything.
Oh, sick, sick!

(Takes the pen and writes.)

Enter Mr. Pinchwife, *who seeing her writing steals softly behind her, and looking over her shoulder, snatches the paper from her.*

PINCHWIFE.

What, writing more letters?

MRS. PINCHWIFE.

O Lord, bud! why d'ye fright me so?   15

(She offers to run out; he stops her, and reads.)

PINCHWIFE.

How's this! Nay, you shall not stir, madam. "Dear, dear, dear Mr. Horner"—very well—I have taught you to write letters to good purpose—but let's see't.

"First, I am to beg your pardon for my boldness in writing to you, which I'd have you to know I would not have done   20
had not you said first you loved me so extremely, which if you do, you will never suffer me to lie in the arms of another man, whom I loathe, nauseate, and detest."—Now you can write these filthy words. But what follows? —"Therefore I hope you will speedily find some way to free me from this   25
unfortunate match, which was never, I assure you, of my choice, but I'm afraid 'tis already too far gone. However, if you love me, as I do you, you will try what you can do, but you must help me away before tomorrow, or else, alas, I shall be forever out of your reach, for I can defer no longer   30
our—our" *(The letter concludes.)*—What is to follow "our"? —Speak, what? Our journey into the country, I suppose— Oh, woman, damned woman! and love, damned love, their old tempter! for this is one of his miracles; in a moment he can make those blind that could see, and those see that were   35
blind, those dumb that could speak, and those prattle who were dumb before; nay, what is more than all, make these dough-baked, senseless, indocile animals, women, too hard for us, their politic lords and rulers, in a moment. But make an end of your letter, and then I'll make an end of you thus,   40

21. not you] *Q1-4, O;* you not *Q5.*

and all my plagues together.

(*Draws his sword.*)

MRS. PINCHWIFE.

O Lord, O Lord, you are such a passionate man, bud!

Enter Sparkish.

SPARKISH.

How now, what's here to do?

PINCHWIFE.

This fool here now!

SPARKISH.

What, drawn upon your wife? You should never do that but   45
at night in the dark, when you can't hurt her. This is my
sister-in-law, is it not?   (*Pulls aside her handkerchief.*)   Ay,
faith, e'en our country Margery; one may know her. Come,
she and you must go dine with me; dinner's ready, come.
But where's my wife? Is she not come home yet? Where is   50
she?

PINCHWIFE.

Making you a cuckold; 'tis that they all do, as soon as they
can.

SPARKISH.

What, the wedding day? No, a wife that designs to make a
cully of her husband will be sure to let him win the first stake   55
of love, by the world. But come, they stay dinner for us;
come, I'll lead down our Margery.

MRS. PINCHWIFE.

No—sir, go, we'll follow you.

SPARKISH.

I will not wag without you.

PINCHWIFE [*aside*].

This coxcomb is a sensible torment to me amidst the   60
greatest in the world.

SPARKISH.

Come, come, Madam Margery.

---

45. drawn] *Q 1–4, O;* draw *Q 5.*   52. all] *Q 1–4, O;* also *Q 5.*
49. dine] *Q 1–4, O;* to dine *Q 5.*   55. cully] *Q 1–4, O;* cuckold *Q 5.*

---

55. *cully*] dupe.   59. *wag*] stir.
60. *sensible*] acutely felt.

PINCHWIFE.

No, I'll lead her my own way. What, would you treat your
friends with mine, for want of your own wife? (*Leads her
to t'other door, and locks her in, and returns.*) —(*Aside.*) I am   65
contented my rage should take breath.

SPARKISH [*aside*].

I told Horner this.

PINCHWIFE.

Come now.

SPARKISH.

Lord, how shy you are of your wife! But let me tell you,
brother, we men of wit have amongst us a saying that   70
cuckolding, like the smallpox, comes with a fear, and you
may keep your wife as much as you will out of danger of
infection, but if her constitution incline her to't, she'll have
it sooner or later, by the world, say they.

PINCHWIFE (*aside*).

What a thing is a cuckold, that every fool can make him   75
ridiculous! —Well, sir—but let me advise you, now you are
come to be concerned, because you suspect the danger, not
to neglect the means to prevent it, especially when the
greatest share of the malady will light upon your own head,
for   80

Hows'e'er the kind wife's belly comes to swell,
The husband breeds for her, and first is ill.

                                  [*Exeunt* Pinchwife *and* Sparkish.]

[V.i]   *Mr. Pinchwife's house.*
     Enter Mr. Pinchwife *and* Mrs. Pinchwife. *A table and candle.*

PINCHWIFE.

Come, take the pen and make an end of the letter, just as
you intended; if you are false in a tittle, I shall soon perceive
it, and punish you with this as you deserve. (*Lays his hand
on his sword.*) Write what was to follow—let's see—"You
must make haste and help me away before tomorrow, or else   5
I shall be forever out of your reach, for I can defer no longer

---

63. own] *Q1–5; om. O.*   79. head] *Q1–4, O;* heads *Q5.*

---

69. *shy*] distrustful.

our"—What follows "our"?

MRS. PINCHWIFE.

Must all out then, bud? (Mrs. Pinchwife *takes the pen and writes.*) Look you there then.

PINCHWIFE.

Let's see—"For I can defer no longer our—wedding— 10
Your slighted Alithea."—What's the meaning of this?
My sister's name to't. Speak, unriddle!

MRS. PINCHWIFE.

Yes, indeed, bud.

PINCHWIFE.

But why her name to't? Speak—speak, I say!

MRS. PINCHWIFE.

Ay, but you'll tell her then again; if you would not tell her 15
again—

PINCHWIFE.

I will not—I am stunned, my head turns round. Speak.

MRS. PINCHWIFE.

Won't you tell her indeed, and indeed?

PINCHWIFE.

No, speak, I say.

MRS. PINCHWIFE.

She'll be angry with me, but I had rather she should be 20
angry with me than you, bud; and to tell you the truth,
'twas she made me write the letter, and taught me what I
should write.

PINCHWIFE (*aside*).

Ha! I thought the style was somewhat better than her own.
—But how could she come to you to teach you, since I had 25
locked you up alone?

MRS. PINCHWIFE.

Oh, through the keyhole, bud.

PINCHWIFE.

But why should she make you write a letter for her to him,
since she can write herself?

MRS. PINCHWIFE.

Why, she said because—for I was unwilling to do it. 30

---

24. (*aside*)] *Q 4–5, O; om. Q 1–3.* 25. But how] *Q 1–3; om. Q 4–5, O.*

PINCHWIFE.

Because what—because?

MRS. PINCHWIFE.

Because, lest Mr. Horner should be cruel, and refuse her;
or vain afterwards, and show the letter, she might disown it,
the hand not being hers.

PINCHWIFE (*aside*).

How's this? Ha! —then I think I shall come to myself   35
again. This changeling could not invent this lie; but if she
could, why should she? She might think I should soon
discover it—stay—now I think on't too, Horner said he was
sorry she had married Sparkish, and her disowning her
marriage to me makes me think she has evaded it for   40
Horner's sake. Yet why should she take this course? But
men in love are fools; women may well be so. —But hark
you, madam, your sister went out in the morning, and I
have not seen her within since.

MRS. PINCHWIFE.

Alackaday, she has been crying all day above, it seems, in a   45
corner.

PINCHWIFE.

Where is she? Let me speak with her.

MRS. PINCHWIFE (*aside*).

O Lord, then he'll discover all! —Pray hold, bud; what,
d'ye mean to discover me? She'll know I have told you then.
Pray, bud, let me talk with her first.   50

PINCHWIFE.

I must speak with her, to know whether Horner ever made
her any promise, and whether she be married to Sparkish
or no.

MRS. PINCHWIFE.

Pray, dear bud, don't, till I have spoken with her and told
her that I have told you all, for she'll kill me else.   55

PINCHWIFE.

Go then, and bid her come out to me.

MRS. PINCHWIFE.

Yes, yes, bud.

48. he'll] *Q 1–5;* she'll *O.*

PINCHWIFE.

Let me see—

MRS. PINCHWIFE [*aside*].

I'll go, but she is not within to come to him. I have just got
time to know of Lucy her maid, who first set me on work,   60
what lie I shall tell next, for I am e'en at my wit's end.

Exit Mrs. Pinchwife.

PINCHWIFE.

Well, I resolve it; Horner shall have her. I'd rather give
him my sister than lend him my wife, and such an alliance
will prevent his pretensions to my wife, sure. I'll make him
of kin to her, and then he won't care for her.   65

Mrs. Pinchwife *returns*.

MRS. PINCHWIFE.

O Lord, bud! I told you what anger you would make me
with my sister.

PINCHWIFE.

Won't she come hither?

MRS. PINCHWIFE.

No, no, alackaday, she's ashamed to look you in the face, and
she says, if you go in to her, she'll run away downstairs, and   70
shamefully go herself to Mr. Horner, who has promised her
marriage, she says, and she will have no other, so she won't.

PINCHWIFE.

Did he so—promise her marriage?—then she shall have no
other. Go tell her so, and if she will come and discourse with
me a little concerning the means, I will about it immediately.   75
Go.   *Exit* Mrs. Pinchwife.

His estate is equal to Sparkish's, and his extraction as much
better than his as his parts are; but my chief reason is, I'd
rather be of kin to him by the name of brother-in-law than
that of cuckold.   80

Enter Mrs. Pinchwife.

Well, what says she now?

MRS. PINCHWIFE.

Why, she says she would only have you lead her to Horner's

80.1. *Enter* Mrs. Pinchwife] Q *1–3;*
om. Q *4–5, O.*

lodging—with whom she first will discourse the matter before
she talks with you, which yet she cannot do; for alack,
poor creature, she says she can't so much as look you in the   85
face, therefore she'll come to you in a mask; and you must
excuse her if she make you no answer to any question of
yours, till you have brought her to Mr. Horner; and if you
will not chide her, nor question her, she'll come out to
you immediately.   90

PINCHWIFE.

Let her come; I will not speak a word to her, nor require a
word from her.

MRS. PINCHWIFE.

Oh, I forgot; besides, she says she cannot look you in the
face though through a mask, therefore would desire you to
put out the candle.   95

PINCHWIFE.

I agree to all; let her make haste—there, 'tis out. (*Puts
out the candle.*)   *Exit* Mrs. Pinchwife.
—My case is something better. I'd rather fight with Horner
for not lying with my sister than for lying with my wife,
and of the two I had rather find my sister too forward than
my wife; I expected no other from her free education, as 100
she calls it, and her passion for the town. Well—wife and
sister are names which make us expect love and duty,
pleasure and comfort, but we find 'em plagues and
torments, and are equally, though differently, troublesome
to their keeper; for we have as much ado to get people to 105
lie with our sisters as to keep 'em from lying with our wives.

Enter Mrs. Pinchwife *masked, and in a hood and scarf and a nightgown and
petticoat of* Alithea's, *in the dark.*

What, are you come, sister? Let us go then—but first let me
lock up my wife. —Mrs. Margery, where are you?

MRS. PINCHWIFE.

Here, bud.

84. talks] *Q 4–5, O;* talk *Q 1–3.*   106.1. *a   hood   and   scarf*]   *Q 5;*
                                              hoods and scarves *Q 1–4, O.*

106.1. *nightgown*] dressing gown.

PINCHWIFE.

Come hither, that I may lock you up; get you in. (*Locks the* 110
door.)—Come, sister, where are you now?

(Mrs. Pinchwife *gives him her hand, but when he lets her go, she steals
softly on t'other side of him, and is led away by him for his sister* Alithea.)

[V.ii] *The scene changes to* Horner's *lodging.* Quack, Horner.

QUACK.

What, all alone? Not so much as one of your cuckolds here,
nor one of their wives! They use to take their turns with you,
as if they were to watch you.

HORNER.

Yes, it often happens that a cuckold is but his wife's spy, and
is more upon family duty when he is with her gallant abroad,   5
hindering his pleasure, than when he is at home with her,
playing the gallant. But the hardest duty a married woman
imposes upon a lover is keeping her husband company
always.

QUACK.

And his fondness wearies you almost as soon as hers.   10

HORNER.

A pox! keeping a cuckold company, after you have had his
wife, is as tiresome as the company of a country squire to a
witty fellow of the town, when he has got all his money.

QUACK.

And as at first a man makes a friend of the husband to get
the wife, so at last you are fain to fall out with the wife to   15
be rid of the husband.

HORNER.

Ay, most cuckold-makers are true courtiers; when once a
poor man has cracked his credit for 'em, they can't abide
to come near him.

QUACK.

But at first, to draw him in, are so sweet, so kind, so dear,   20
just as you are to Pinchwife. But what becomes of that
intrigue with his wife?

HORNER.

A pox! he's as surly as an alderman that has been bit, and

111.1. steals] *Q 1–5; steal O.*

since he's so coy, his wife's kindness is in vain, for she's a
silly innocent.   25

QUACK.

Did she not send you a letter by him?

HORNER.

Yes, but that's a riddle I have not yet solved. Allow the
poor creature to be willing, she is silly too, and he keeps
her up so close—

QUACK.

Yes, so close that he makes her but the more willing, and   30
adds but revenge to her love, which two, when met, seldom
fail of satisfying each other one way or other.

HORNER.

What! here's the man we are talking of, I think.

Enter Mr. Pinchwife, *leading in his wife masked, muffled, and in her
sister's gown.*

Pshaw!

QUACK.

Bringing his wife to you is the next thing to bringing a love   35
letter from her.

HORNER.

What means this?

PINCHWIFE.

The last time, you know, sir, I brought you a love letter;
now, you see, a mistress. I think you'll say I am a civil man
to you.   40

HORNER.

Ay, the devil take me, will I say thou art the civilest man I
ever met with, and I have known some. I fancy I understand
thee now better than I did the letter; but hark thee, in thy
ear—

PINCHWIFE.

What?   45

HORNER.

Nothing but the usual question, man: is she sound, on thy
word?

41. will I] *Q1–4, O;* I will *Q5.*

PINCHWIFE.

What, you take her for a wench, and me for a pimp?

HORNER.

Pshaw! wench and pimp, paw words. I know thou art an
honest fellow, and hast a great acquaintance among the   50
ladies, and perhaps hast made love for me rather than let
me make love to thy wife.

PINCHWIFE.

Come, sir, in short, I am for no fooling.

HORNER.

Nor I neither; therefore prithee let's see her face presently.
Make her show, man; art thou sure I don't know her?   55

PINCHWIFE.

I am sure you do know her.

HORNER.

A pox! why dost thou bring her to me then?

PINCHWIFE.

Because she's a relation of mine—

HORNER.

Is she, faith, man? Then thou art still more civil and
obliging, dear rogue.   60

PINCHWIFE.

Who desired me to bring her to you.

HORNER.

Then she is obliging, dear rogue.

PINCHWIFE.

You'll make her welcome for my sake, I hope.

HORNER.

I hope she is handsome enough to make herself welcome.
Prithee, let her unmask.   65

PINCHWIFE.

Do you speak to her; she would never be ruled by me.

HORNER.

Madam—(Mrs. Pinchwife *whispers to* Horner.) ·—She says
she must speak with me in private.   Withdraw, prithee.

PINCHWIFE (*aside*).

She's unwilling, it seems, I should know all her undecent

---

49. *paw*] improper, naughty.

conduct in this business. —Well then, I'll leave you together,   70
and hope when I am gone you'll agree; if not, you and I
shan't agree, sir.

HORNER [*aside*].

What means the fool? —If she and I agree, 'tis no matter
what you and I do.

(*Whispers to* Mrs. Pinchwife, *who makes signs with her hand for him*
[Pinchwife] *to be gone.*)

PINCHWIFE.

In the meantime, I'll fetch a parson, and find out Sparkish   75
and disabuse him. You would have me fetch a parson,
would you not? Well then—now I think I am rid of her,
and shall have no more trouble with her. Our sisters and
daughters, like usurers' money, are safest when put out;
but our wives, like their writings, never safe but in our   80
closets under lock and key.

Exit Mr. Pinchwife.

Enter Boy.

BOY.

Sir·Jasper Fidget, sir, is coming up.   [*Exit.*]

HORNER.

Here's the trouble of a cuckold, now, we are talking of.
A pox on him! Has he not enough to do to hinder his wife's
sport, but he must other women's too? —Step in here,   85
madam.   *Exit* Mrs. Pinchwife.

Enter Sir Jasper.

SIR JASPER FIDGET.

My best and dearest friend.

HORNER [*aside to* Quack].

The old style, doctor. —Well, be short, for I am busy.
What would your impertinent wife have now?

SIR JASPER FIDGET.

Well guessed, i'faith, for I do come from her.   90

HORNER.

To invite me to supper. Tell her I can't come; go.

74.1. hand] *Q1–4, O;* hands *Q5.*
84. Has he] *Q1–4, O;* He has *Q5.*

80. *writings*] legal documents, especially deeds.

SIR JASPER FIDGET.

    Nay, now you are out, faith; for my lady and the whole knot
of the virtuous gang, as they call themselves, are resolved
upon a frolic of coming to you tonight in a masquerade, and
are all dressed already.   95

HORNER.

    I shan't be at home.

SIR JASPER FIDGET [*aside*].

    Lord, how churlish he is to women! —Nay, prithee don't
disappoint 'em; they'll think 'tis my fault; prithee don't.
I'll send in the banquet and the fiddles. But make no noise
on't, for the poor virtuous rogues would not have it known 100
for the world that they go a-masquerading, and they would
come to no man's ball but yours.

HORNER.

    Well, well—get you gone, and tell 'em, if they come, 'twill
be at the peril of their honor and yours.

SIR JASPER FIDGET.

    He, he, he!—we'll trust you for that; farewell.   105

                                  Exit Sir Jasper.

HORNER.

    Doctor, anon you too shall be my guest,
But now I'm going to a private feast.   [*Exeunt.*]

[V.iii]   *The scene changes to the Piazza of Covent Garden.*
                Sparkish, Pinchwife.

SPARKISH (*with the letter in his hand*).

    But who would have thought a woman could have been
false to me? By the world, I could not have thought it.

PINCHWIFE.

    You were for giving and taking liberty; she has taken it only,
sir, now you find in that letter. You are a frank person,
and so is she, you see there.   5

SPARKISH.

    Nay, if this be her hand—for I never saw it.

---

94. a masquerade] *Q1–3;* mas-   104. honor] *Q1–4, O;* honors *Q5.*
querade *Q4–5, O.*

1. *S.D. letter*] written by Mrs. Pinchwife.

PINCHWIFE.

'Tis no matter whether that be her hand or no; I am sure
this hand, at her desire, led her to Mr. Horner, with whom
I left her just now, to go fetch a parson to 'em, at their
desire too, to deprive you of her forever, for it seems yours   10
was but a mock marriage.

SPARKISH.

Indeed, she would needs have it that 'twas Harcourt
himself in a parson's habit that married us, but I'm sure he
told me 'twas his brother Ned.

PINCHWIFE.

Oh, there 'tis out, and you were deceived, not she, for you   15
are such a frank person—but I must be gone. You'll find
her at Mr. Horner's; go and believe your eyes.

Exit Mr. Pinchwife.

SPARKISH.

Nay, I'll to her, and call her as many crocodiles, sirens,
harpies, and other heathenish names as a poet would do a
mistress who had refused to hear his suit, nay more, his   20
verses on her. —But stay, is not that she following a torch
at t'other end of the Piazza? And from Horner's certainly—
'tis so.

Enter Alithea, following a torch, and Lucy behind.

You are well met, madam, though you don't think so. What,
you have made a short visit to Mr. Horner, but I suppose   25
you'll return to him presently; by that time the parson can
be with him.

ALITHEA.

Mr. Horner, and the parson, sir!

SPARKISH.

Come, madam, no more dissembling, no more jilting, for I
am no more a frank person.   30

ALITHEA.

How's this?

LUCY (*aside*).

So, 'twill work, I see.

9. fetch] *Q 1–4, O;* to fetch *Q 5.*

21. *torch*] linkboy with torch.

SPARKISH.

> Could you find out no easy country fool to abuse? none but
> me, a gentleman of wit and pleasure about the town?
> But it was your pride to be too hard for a man of parts,   35
> unworthy false woman! false as a friend that lends a man
> money to lose; false as dice, who undo those that trust all
> they have to 'em.

LUCY (*aside*).

> He has been a great bubble by his similes, as they say.

ALITHEA.

> You have been too merry, sir, at your wedding dinner, sure.   40

SPARKISH.

> What, d'ye mock me too?

ALITHEA.

> Or you have been deluded.

SPARKISH.

> By you.

ALITHEA.

> Let me understand you.

SPARKISH.

> Have you the confidence—I should call it something else,   45
> since you know your guilt—to stand my just reproaches?
> You did not write an impudent letter to Mr. Horner! who
> I find now has clubbed with you in deluding me with his
> aversion for women, that I might not, forsooth, suspect him
> for my rival.   50

LUCY (*aside*).

> D'ye think the gentleman can be jealous now, madam?

ALITHEA.

> I write a letter to Mr. Horner!

SPARKISH.

> Nay, madam, do not deny it; your brother showed it me
> just now, and told me likewise he left you at Horner's
> lodging to fetch a parson to marry you to him, and I wish you   55
> joy, madam, joy, joy! and to him, too, much joy, and to
> myself more joy for not marrying you.

ALITHEA (*aside*).

> So, I find my brother would break off the match, and I
> can consent to't, since I see this gentleman can be made
> jealous. —O Lucy, by his rude usage and jealousy, he makes   60
> me almost afraid I am married to him. Art thou sure 'twas

Harcourt himself and no parson that married us?

SPARKISH.

No, madam, I thank you. I suppose that was a contrivance
too of Mr. Horner's and yours, to make Harcourt play the
parson; but I would as little as you have him one now, no,   65
not for the world, for shall I tell you another truth? I never
had any passion for you till now, for now I hate you. 'Tis
true I might have married your portion, as other men of
parts of the town do sometimes, and so your servant; and to
show my unconcernedness, I'll come to your wedding, and   70
resign you with as much joy as I would a stale wench to a
new cully; nay, with as much joy as I would after the first
night, if I had been married to you. There's for you, and
so your servant, servant.   *Exit* Sparkish.

ALITHEA.

How was I deceived in a man!   75

LUCY.

You'll believe, then, a fool may be made jealous now?
For that easiness in him that suffers him to be led by a wife
will likewise permit him to be persuaded against her by
others.

ALITHEA.

But marry Mr. Horner! My brother does not intend it, sure;   80
if I thought he did, I would take thy advice, and Mr.
Harcourt for my husband. And now I wish that if there be
any over-wise woman of the town, who, like me, would
marry a fool for fortune, liberty, or title, first, that her
husband may love play, and be a cully to all the town but   85
her, and suffer none but fortune to be mistress of his purse;
then, if for liberty, that he may send her into the country
under the conduct of some housewifely mother-in-law; and
if for title, may the world give 'em none but that of cuckold.

LUCY.

And for her greater curse, madam, may he not deserve it.   90

ALITHEA.

Away, impertinent! —Is not this my old Lady Lanterlu's?

LUCY.

Yes, madam. —(*Aside.*)   And here I hope we shall find
Mr. Harcourt.   *Exeunt* Alithea, Lucy.

---

91. *Lady Lanterlu's*] from the card game, lanterloo, or loo.

[V.iv]

The scene changes again to Horner's *lodging.* Horner, Lady Fidget,
Mrs. Dainty Fidget, Mrs. Squeamish. *A table, banquet, and bottles.*

HORNER (*aside*).

A pox! they are come too soon—before I have sent back my
new mistress. All I have now to do is to lock her in, that they
may not see her.

LADY FIDGET.

That we may be sure of our welcome, we have brought our
entertainment with us, and are resolved to treat thee, dear   5
toad.

MRS. DAINTY FIDGET.

And that we may be merry to purpose, have left Sir Jasper
and my old Lady Squeamish quarreling at home at
backgammon.

MRS. SQUEAMISH.

Therefore let us make use of our time, lest they should   10
chance to interrupt us.

LADY FIDGET.

Let us sit then.

HORNER.

First, that you may be private, let me lock this door and
that, and I'll wait upon you presently.

LADY FIDGET.

No, sir, shut 'em only and your lips forever, for we must trust   15
you as much as our women.

HORNER.

You know all vanity's killed in me; I have no occasion for
talking.

LADY FIDGET.

Now, ladies, supposing we had drank each of us our two
bottles, let us speak the truth of our hearts.   20

MRS. DAINTY FIDGET AND MRS. SQUEAMISH.

Agreed.

LADY FIDGET.

By this brimmer, for truth is nowhere else to be found.
—(*Aside to* Horner.)   Not in thy heart, false man!

4. brought our] *Q1–4, O;* brought
an *Q5.*

HORNER (*aside to* Lady Fidget).

    You have found me a true man, I'm sure.

LADY FIDGET (*aside to* Horner).

    Not every way. —But let us sit and be merry.   25

                (Lady Fidget *sings*.)

                      1

    Why should our damn'd tyrants oblige us to live

    On the pittance of pleasure which they only give?

        We must not rejoice,

        With wine and with noise.

    In vain we must wake in a dull bed alone,   30

    Whilst to our warm rival, the bottle, they're gone.

        Then lay aside charms,

        And take up these arms.*   (* *The glasses*.)

                      2

    'Tis wine only gives 'em their courage and wit;

    Because we live sober, to men we submit.   35

        If for beauties you'd pass,

        Take a lick of the glass,

    'Twill mend your complexions, and when they are gone,

    The best red we have is the red of the grape.

        Then, sisters, lay't on,   40

        And damn a good shape.

MRS. DAINTY FIDGET.

    Dear brimmer! Well, in token of our openness and plain-
dealing, let us throw our masks over our heads.

HORNER.

    So, 'twill come to the glasses anon.

MRS. SQUEAMISH.

    Lovely brimmer! Let me enjoy him first.   45

LADY FIDGET.

    No, I never part with a gallant till I've tried him. Dear
brimmer, that mak'st our husbands shortsighted.

MRS. DAINTY FIDGET.

    And our bashful gallants bold.

MRS. SQUEAMISH.

    And for want of a gallant, the butler lovely in our eyes.
—Drink, eunuch.   50

LADY FIDGET.

Drink, thou representative of a husband. Damn a husband!

MRS. DAINTY FIDGET.

And, as it were a husband, an old keeper.

MRS. SQUEAMISH.

And an old grandmother.

HORNER.

And an English bawd, and a French surgeon.

LADY FIDGET.

Ay, we have all reason to curse 'em.   55

HORNER.

For my sake, ladies?

LADY FIDGET.

No, for our own, for the first spoils all young gallants' industry.

MRS. DAINTY FIDGET.

And the other's art makes 'em bold only with common women.   60

MRS. SQUEAMISH.

And rather run the hazard of the vile distemper amongst them than of a denial amongst us.

MRS. DAINTY FIDGET.

The filthy toads choose mistresses now as they do stuffs, for having been fancied and worn by others.

MRS. SQUEAMISH.

For being common and cheap.   65

LADY FIDGET.

Whilst women of quality, like the richest stuffs, lie untumbled and unasked for.

HORNER.

Ay, neat, and cheap, and new, often they think best.

MRS. DAINTY FIDGET.

No, sir, the beasts will be known by a mistress longer than by a suit.   70

MRS. SQUEAMISH.

And 'tis not for cheapness neither.

---

54. *French surgeon*] doctor for venereal disease.

LADY FIDGET.

No, for the vain fops will take up druggets and embroider
'em. But I wonder at the depraved appetites of witty men;
they use to be out of the common road, and hate imitation.
Pray tell me, beast, when you were a man, why you rather   75
chose to club with a multitude in a common house for an
entertainment than to be the only guest at a good table.

HORNER.

Why, faith, ceremony and expectation are unsufferable to
those that are sharp bent; people always eat with the best
stomach at an ordinary, where every man is snatching for the   80
best bit.

LADY FIDGET.

Though he get a cut over the fingers. —But I have heard
people eat most heartily of another man's meat, that is,
what they do not pay for.

HORNER.

When they are sure of their welcome and freedom, for   85
ceremony in love and eating is as ridiculous as in fighting;
falling on briskly is all should be done in those occasions.

LADY FIDGET.

Well, then, let me tell you, sir, there is nowhere more
freedom than in our houses, and we take freedom from a
young person as a sign of good breeding, and a person may   90
be as free as he pleases with us, as frolic, as gamesome, as
wild as he will.

HORNER.

Han't I heard you all declaim against wild men?

LADY FIDGET.

Yes, but for all that, we think wildness in a man as desirable
a quality as in a duck or rabbit; a tame man, foh!   95

HORNER.

I know not, but your reputations frightened me, as much
as your faces invited me.

LADY FIDGET.

Our reputation! Lord, why should you not think that we
women make use of our reputation, as you men of yours,

---

72. *druggets*] inexpensive woolen material.
76. *common house*] ordinary; also bawdy house.

only to deceive the world with less suspicion? Our virtue 100
is like the statesman's religion, the Quaker's word, the
gamester's oath, and the great man's honor—but to cheat
those that trust us.

MRS. SQUEAMISH.

And that demureness, coyness, and modesty that you see in
our faces in the boxes at plays, is as much a sign of a kind 105
woman as a vizard-mask in the pit.

MRS. DAINTY FIDGET.

For, I assure you, women are least masked when they have
the velvet vizard on.

LADY FIDGET.

You would have found us modest women in our denials
only.   110

MRS. SQUEAMISH.

Our bashfulness is only the reflection of the men's.

MRS. DAINTY FIDGET.

We blush when they are shamefaced.

HORNER.

I beg your pardon, ladies; I was deceived in you devilishly.
But why that mighty pretense to honor?

LADY FIDGET.

We have told you. But sometimes 'twas for the same reason 115
you men pretend business often, to avoid ill company, to
enjoy the better and more privately those you love.

HORNER.

But why would you ne'er give a friend a wink then?

LADY FIDGET.

Faith, your reputation frightened us as much as ours did
you, you were so notoriously lewd.   120

HORNER.

And you so seemingly honest.

LADY FIDGET.

Was that all that deterred you?

HORNER.

And so expensive—you allow freedom, you say—

---

101. statesman's] *Q1–4, O;* states-   111. reflection] *Q1–4, O;* reflections
men's *Q5.*   *Q5.*

---

106. *vizard-mask*] sign of a whore.   121. *honest*] chaste.

LADY FIDGET.

Ay, ay.

HORNER.

That I was afraid of losing my little money, as well as my 125
little time, both which my other pleasures required.

LADY FIDGET.

Money, foh! You talk like a little fellow now; do such as we
expect money?

HORNER.

I beg your pardon, madam; I must confess, I have heard
that great ladies, like great merchants, set but the higher 130
prices upon what they have, because they are not in
necessity of taking the first offer.

MRS. DAINTY FIDGET.

Such as we make sale of our hearts?

MRS. SQUEAMISH.

We bribed for our love? Foh!

HORNER.

With your pardon, ladies, I know, like great men in offices, 135
you seem to exact flattery and attendance only from your
followers; but you have receivers about you, and such fees
to pay, a man is afraid to pass your grants. Besides, we must
let you win at cards, or we lose your hearts; and if you
make an assignation, 'tis at a goldsmith's, jeweler's, or china 140
house, where, for your honor you deposit to him, he must
pawn his to the punctual cit, and so paying for what you
take up, pays for what he takes up.

MRS. DAINTY FIDGET.

Would you not have us assured of our gallant's love?

MRS. SQUEAMISH.

For love is better known by liberality than by jealousy.   145

LADY FIDGET.

For one may be dissembled, the other not. —(*Aside.*)   But

---

131. prices] *prizes Q 1–5, O.*   132. offer] *Q 1–4, O; om. Q 5.*

137. *receivers*] servants to be bribed.
138. *to pass your grants*] to accept your favors.
141–143. *for your honor . . . takes up*] for putting your honor in the gallant's
hands, he must pawn his honor to the goldsmith, and so paying for what
you obtain, the gallant pays for what he obtains.

my jealousy can be no longer dissembled, and they are telling ripe. —Come, here's to our gallants in waiting, whom we must name, and I'll begin. This is my false rogue.

(Claps him on the back.)

MRS. SQUEAMISH.

How! 150

HORNER [*aside*].

So, all will out now.

MRS. SQUEAMISH (*aside to* Horner).

Did you not tell me, 'twas for my sake only you reported yourself no man?

MRS. DAINTY FIDGET (*aside to* Horner).

Oh, wretch! Did you not swear to me, 'twas for my love and honor you passed for that thing you do? 155

HORNER.

So, so.

LADY FIDGET.

Come, speak, ladies; this is my false villain.

MRS. SQUEAMISH.

And mine too.

MRS. DAINTY FIDGET.

And mine.

HORNER.

Well then, you are all three my false rogues too, and there's 160 an end on't.

LADY FIDGET.

Well then, there's no remedy; sister sharers, let us not fall out, but have a care of our honor. Though we get no presents, no jewels of him, we are savers of our honor, the jewel of most value and use, which shines yet to the world 165 unsuspected, though it be counterfeit.

HORNER.

Nay, and is e'en as good as if it were true, provided the world think so; for honor, like beauty now, only depends on the opinion of others.

LADY FIDGET.

Well, Harry Common, I hope you can be true to three. 170 Swear—but 'tis to no purpose to require your oath, for you

147. jealousy] *Q1–2, 4–5, O;* jealousies *Q3.* 167. if] *Q1–4, O; om. Q5.*
171. to no] *Q2–5, O;* no *Q1.*

are as often forsworn as you swear to new women.

HORNER.

Come, faith, madam, let us e'en pardon one another, for all
the difference I find betwixt we men and you women, we
forswear ourselves at the beginning of an amour, you as long 175
as it lasts.

Enter Sir Jasper Fidget, *and* Old Lady Squeamish.

SIR JASPER FIDGET.

Oh, my Lady Fidget, was this your cunning, to come to
Mr. Horner without me? But you have been nowhere else,
I hope.

LADY FIDGET.

No, Sir Jasper.   180

OLD LADY SQUEAMISH.

And you came straight hither, Biddy?

MRS. SQUEAMISH.

Yes, indeed, Lady Grandmother.

SIR JASPER FIDGET.

'Tis well, 'tis well; I knew when once they were thoroughly
acquainted with poor Horner, they'd ne'er be from him.
You may let her masquerade it with my wife and Horner, 185
and I warrant her reputation safe.

Enter Boy.

BOY.

Oh, sir, here's the gentleman come whom you bid me not
suffer to come up without giving you notice, with a lady
too, and other gentlemen.

HORNER.

Do you all go in there, whilst I send 'em away, and, boy, 190
do you desire 'em to stay below till I come, which shall be
immediately.

Exeunt Sir Jasper, [Old] Lady Squeamish, Lady Fidget, Mrs. Dainty,
[Mrs.] Squeamish.

BOY.

Yes, sir.   *Exit.*

        Exit Horner *at t'other door, and returns with* Mrs. Pinchwife.

HORNER.

You would not take my advice to be gone home before your

husband came back; he'll now discover all. Yet pray, my 195
dearest, be persuaded to go home, and leave the rest to my
management; I'll let you down the back way.

MRS. PINCHWIFE.

I don't know the way home, so I don't.

HORNER.

My man shall wait upon you.

MRS. PINCHWIFE.

No, don't you believe that I'll go at all; what, are you 200
weary of me already?

HORNER.

No, my life, 'tis that I may love you long, 'tis to secure my
love, and your reputation with your husband; he'll never
receive you again else.

MRS. PINCHWIFE.

What care I? D'ye think to frighten me with that? I don't 205
intend to go to him again; you shall be my husband now.

HORNER.

I cannot be your husband, dearest, since you are married
to him.

MRS. PINCHWIFE.

Oh, would you make me believe that? Don't I see every day,
at London here, women leave their first husbands, and go 210
and live with other men as their wives? Pish, pshaw! you'd
make me angry, but that I love you so mainly.

HORNER.

So, they are coming up—in again, in, I hear 'em.

Exit Mrs. Pinchwife.

Well, a silly mistress is like a weak place, soon got, soon lost,
a man has scarce time for plunder; she betrays her husband 215
first to her gallant, and then her gallant to her husband.

Enter Pinchwife, Alithea, Harcourt, Sparkish, Lucy, *and a* Parson.

PINCHWIFE.

Come, madam, 'tis not the sudden change of your dress, the
confidence of your asseverations, and your false witness
there, shall persuade me I did not bring you hither just now;

209. would you] *Q1-4, O;* you
would *Q5.*

---

212. *mainly*] strongly, much.

here's my witness, who cannot deny it, since you must be 220
confronted. —Mr. Horner, did not I bring this lady to you
just now?

HORNER (*aside*).

Now must I wrong one woman for another's sake, but that's
no new thing with me; for in these cases I am still on the
criminal's side, against the innocent.   225

ALITHEA.

Pray, speak, sir.

HORNER (*aside*).

It must be so—I must be impudent, and try my luck;
impudence uses to be too hard for truth.

PINCHWIFE.

What, you are studying an evasion or excuse for her.
Speak, sir.   230

HORNER.

No, faith, I am something backward only to speak in
women's affairs, or disputes.

PINCHWIFE.

She bids you speak.

ALITHEA.

Ay, pray, sir, do; pray satisfy him.

HORNER.

Then truly, you did bring that lady to me just now.   235

PINCHWIFE.

O ho!

ALITHEA.

How, sir!

HARCOURT.

How, Horner!

ALITHEA.

What mean you, sir? I always took you for a man of honor.

HORNER (*aside*).

Ay, so much a man of honor that I must save my mistress, 240
I thank you, come what will on't.

SPARKISH.

So, if I had had her, she'd have made me believe the moon
had been made of a Christmas pie.

232. women's] *Q1-4, O;* woman's
Q5.

LUCY (*aside*).

 Now could I speak, if I durst, and solve the riddle, who am
 the author of it.   245

ALITHEA.

 O unfortunate woman! A combination against my honor,
 which most concerns me now, because you share in my
 disgrace, sir, and it is your censure, which I must now suffer,
 that troubles me, not theirs.

HARCOURT.

 Madam, then have no trouble, you shall now see 'tis 250
 possible for me to love too, without being jealous; I will
 not only believe your innocence myself, but make all the
 world believe it. —(*Apart to* Horner.) Horner, I must now
 be concerned for this lady's honor.

HORNER.

 And I must be concerned for a lady's honor too.   255

HARCOURT.

 This lady has her honor, and I will protect it.

HORNER.

 My lady has not her honor, but has given it me to keep, and
 I will preserve it.

HARCOURT.

 I understand you not.

HORNER.

 I would not have you.   260

MRS. PINCHWIFE (*peeping in behind*).

 What's the matter with 'em all?

PINCHWIFE.

 Come, come, Mr. Horner, no more disputing; here's the
 parson, I brought him not in vain.

HARCOURT.

 No, sir, I'll employ him, if this lady please.

PINCHWIFE.

 How! what d'ye mean?   265

SPARKISH.

 Ay, what does he mean?

264. S. P. HARCOURT] *Q5;* HORNER
Q1-4, O.

HORNER.

Why, I have resigned your sister to him; he has my consent.

PINCHWIFE.

But he has not mine, sir; a woman's injured honor, no more
than a man's, can be repaired or satisfied by any but him
that first wronged it; and you shall marry her presently, or— 270
                                    (*Lays his hand on his sword.*)

Enter to them Mrs. Pinchwife.

MRS. PINCHWIFE [*aside*].

O Lord, they'll kill poor Mr. Horner! Besides, he shan't
marry her whilst I stand by and look on; I'll not lose my
second husband so.

PINCHWIFE.

What do I see?

ALITHEA.

My sister in my clothes!   275

SPARKISH.

Ha!

MRS. PINCHWIFE (*to* Mr. Pinchwife).

Nay, pray now don't quarrel about finding work for the
parson; he shall marry me to Mr. Horner; for now, I
believe, you have enough of me.

HORNER [*aside*].

Damned, damned, loving changeling!   280

MRS. PINCHWIFE.

Pray, sister, pardon me for telling so many lies of you.

HARCOURT.

I suppose the riddle is plain now.

LUCY.

No, that must be my work. Good sir, hear me.

(*Kneels to* Mr. Pinchwife, *who stands doggedly, with his hat over his eyes.*)

PINCHWIFE.

I will never hear woman again, but make 'em all silent,
thus—   285
                                    (*Offers to draw upon his wife.*)

HORNER.

No, that must not be.

–135–

PINCHWIFE.

You then shall go first, 'tis all one to me.

(*Offers to draw on* Horner; *stopped by* Harcourt.)

HARCOURT.

Hold!

Enter Sir Jasper Fidget, Lady Fidget, [Old] Lady Squeamish, Mrs. Dainty Fidget, Mrs. Squeamish.

SIR JASPER FIDGET.

What's the matter? what's the matter? pray, what's the
matter, sir? I beseech you communicate, sir. 290

PINCHWIFE.

Why, my wife has communicated, sir, as your wife may
have done too, sir, if she knows him, sir.

SIR JASPER FIDGET.

Pshaw! with him! Ha, ha, he!

PINCHWIFE.

D'ye mock me, sir? A cuckold is a kind of a wild beast; have
a care, sir. 295

SIR JASPER FIDGET.

No, sure, you mock me, sir—he cuckold you! It can't be,
ha, ha, he! Why, I'll tell you, sir—

(*Offers to whisper.*)

PINCHWIFE.

I tell you again, he has whored my wife, and yours too, if
he knows her, and all the women he comes near; 'tis not
his dissembling, his hypocrisy, can wheedle me. 300

SIR JASPER FIDGET.

How! does he dissemble? Is he a hypocrite? Nay, then—
how—wife—sister, is he an hypocrite?

OLD LADY SQUEAMISH.

An hypcrite! a dissembler! Speak, young harlotry, speak,
how?

SIR JASPER FIDGET.

Nay, then—oh, my head too! —O thou libidinous lady! 305

OLD LADY SQUEAMISH.

O thou harloting harlotry! Hast thou done't then?

288.1. Lady Fidget] *Q1; om. Q2–5,
O.*
301. a hypocrite] *Q1–4, O;* hypocrite *Q5.*

305. my] *Q1, 3, 5;* my, my *Q2, 4
O.*
306. done't then?] *Q1–3, 5, O; om.
Q4.*

SIR JASPER FIDGET.

Speak, good Horner, art thou a dissembler, a rogue? Hast thou—

HORNER.

Soh!

LUCY (*apart to* Horner).

I'll fetch you off, and her too, if she will but hold her tongue. 310

HORNER (*apart to* Lucy).

Canst thou? I'll give thee—

LUCY (*to* Mr. Pinchwife).

Pray have but patience to hear me, sir, who am the unfortunate cause of all this confusion. Your wife is innocent, I only culpable; for I put her upon telling you all these lies concerning my mistress, in order to the breaking off the 315 match between Mr. Sparkish and her, to make way for Mr. Harcourt.

SPARKISH.

Did you so, eternal rotten tooth? Then, it seems, my mistress was not false to me, I was only deceived by you. —Brother that should have been, now, man of conduct, who 320 is a frank person now? to bring your wife to her lover—ha!

LUCY.

I assure you, sir, she came not to Mr. Horner out of love, for she loves him no more—

MRS. PINCHWIFE.

Hold, I told lies for you, but you shall tell none for me, for I do love Mr. Horner with all my soul, and nobody shall 325 say me nay; pray, don't you go to make poor Mr. Horner believe to the contrary, 'tis spitefully done of you, I'm sure.

HORNER (*aside to* Mrs. Pinchwife).

Peace, dear idiot.

MRS. PINCHWIFE.

Nay, I will not peace.

PINCHWIFE.

Not till I make you. 330

Enter Dorilant, Quack.

DORILANT.

Horner, your servant; I am the doctor's guest, he must

312. but   patience]   *Q 1-4,   O;*
patience but *Q 5.*

excuse our intrusion.

QUACK.

But what's the matter, gentlemen? For heaven's sake, what's the matter?

HORNER.

Oh, 'tis well you are come. 'Tis a censorious world we live 335 in; you may have brought me a reprieve, or else I had died for a crime I never committed, and these innocent ladies had suffered with me; therefore pray satisfy these worthy, honorable, jealous gentlemen—that—

(Whispers.)

QUACK.

Oh, I understand you; is that all? —(*Whispers* to Sir 340 Jasper.) Sir Jasper, by heavens and upon the word of a physician, sir—

SIR JASPER FIDGET.

Nay, I do believe you truly. —Pardon me, my virtuous lady, and dear of honor.

OLD LADY SQUEAMISH.

What, then all's right again?   345

SIR JASPER FIDGET.

Ay, ay, and now let us satisfy him too.

(They whisper with Mr. Pinchwife.)

PINCHWIFE.

An eunuch! Pray, no fooling with me.

QUACK.

I'll bring half the surgeons in town to swear it.

PINCHWIFE.

They!—they'll swear a man that bled to death through his wounds died of an apoplexy.   350

QUACK.

Pray hear me, sir—why, all the town has heard the report of him.

PINCHWIFE.

But does all the town believe it?

QUACK.

Pray inquire a little, and first of all these.

PINCHWIFE.

I'm sure when I left the town he was the lewdest fellow in't. 355

QUACK.

I tell you, sir, he has been in France since; pray ask but

these ladies and gentlemen, your friend Mr. Dorilant.
—Gentlemen and ladies, han't you all heard the late sad
report of poor Mr. Horner?

ALL THE LADIES.

Ay, ay, ay.   360

DORILANT.

Why, thou jealous fool, dost thou doubt it? He's an arrant
French capon.

MRS. PINCHWIFE.

'Tis false, sir, you shall not disparage poor Mr. Horner,
for to my certain knowledge—

LUCY.

Oh, hold!   365

MRS. SQUEAMISH (*aside to* Lucy).

Stop her mouth!

LADY FIDGET (*to* Pinchwife).

Upon my honor, sir, 'tis as true—

MRS. DAINTY FIDGET.

D'ye think we would have been seen in his company?

MRS. SQUEAMISH.

Trust our unspotted reputations with him!

LADY FIDGET (*aside to* Horner).

This you get, and we too, by trusting your secret to a fool. 370

HORNER.

Peace, madam. —(*Aside to* Quack.)   Well, doctor, is not this
a good design, that carries a man on unsuspected, and
brings him off safe?

PINCHWIFE (*aside*).

Well, if this were true, but my wife—

                          (Dorilant *whispers with* Mrs. Pinchwife.)

ALITHEA.

Come, brother, your wife is yet innocent, you see; but have 375
a care of too strong an imagination, lest like an overcon-
cerned, timorous gamester, by fancying an unlucky cast, it
should come. Women and fortune are truest still to those
that trust 'em.

LUCY.,

And any wild thing grows but the more fierce and hungry 380
for being kept up, and more dangerous to the keeper.

---

362. *French capon*] impotent person.

ALITHEA.

There's doctrine for all husbands, Mr. Harcourt.

HARCOURT.

I edify, madam, so much that I am impatient till I am one.

DORILANT.

And I edify so much by example I will never be one.

SPARKISH.

And because I will not disparage my parts I'll ne'er be one. 385

HORNER.

And I, alas, can't be one.

PINCHWIFE.

But I must be one—against my will, to a country wife, with
a country murrain to me.

MRS. PINCHWIFE (*aside*).

And I must be a country wife still too, I find, for I can't,
like a city one, be rid of my musty husband and do what I 390
list.

HORNER.

Now, sir, I must pronounce your wife innocent, though I
blush whilst I do it, and I am the only man by her now
exposed to shame, which I will straight drown in wine, as
you shall your suspicion, and the ladies' troubles we'll divert 395
with a ballet. —Doctor, where are your maskers?

LUCY.

Indeed, she's innocent, sir, I am her witness; and her end of
coming out was but to see her sister's wedding, and what
she has said to your face of her love to Mr. Horner was but
the usual innocent revenge on a husband's jealousy—was 400
it not, madam? Speak.

MRS. PINCHWIFE (*aside to* Lucy *and* Horner).

Since you'll have me tell more lies—Yes, indeed, bud.

PINCHWIFE.

For my own sake fain I would all believe;
Cuckolds, like lovers, should themselves deceive.
But—(*Sighs.*)   405
His honor is least safe, too late I find,
Who trusts it with a foolish wife or friend.

393. whilst] *Q 1-4, O;* while *Q 5.*

---

388. *murrain*] cattle plague.

(*A dance of cuckolds.*)

HORNER.

    Vain fops but court, and dress, and keep a pother,
    To pass for women's men with one another;
    But he who aims by women to be priz'd,   410
    First by the men, you see, must be despis'd.

Finis.

Epilogue
Spoken by Mrs. Knep.

Now, you the vigorous, who daily here ⎫
O'er vizard-mask in public domineer, ⎬
And what you'd do to her if in place where; ⎭
Nay, have the confidence to cry, "Come out!"
Yet when she says, "Lead on," you are not stout;   5
But to your well-dress'd brother straight turn round
And cry, "Pox on her, Ned, she can't be sound!"
Then slink away, a fresh one to engage, ⎫
With so much seeming heat and loving rage, ⎬
You'd frighten listening actress on the stage; ⎭   10
Till she at last has seen you huffing come, ⎫
And talk of keeping in the tiring-room, ⎬
Yet cannot be provok'd to lead her home. ⎭
Next, you Falstaffs of fifty, who beset
Your buckram maidenheads, which your friends get;   15
And whilst to them you of achievements boast,
They share the booty, and laugh at your cost.
In fine, you essenc'd boys, both old and young, ⎫
Who would be thought so eager, brisk, and strong, ⎬
Yet do the ladies, not their husbands, wrong; ⎭   20
Whose purses for your manhood make excuse,
And keep your Flanders mares for show, not use;
Encourag'd by our woman's man today,
A Horner's part may vainly think to play;
And may intrigues so bashfully disown   25
That they may doubted be by few or none;
May kiss the cards at picquet, ombre, loo, ⎫
And so be thought to kiss the lady too; ⎬
But, gallants, have a care, faith, what you do. ⎭
The world, which to no man his due will give,   30
You by experience know you can deceive,
And men may still believe you vigorous,
But then we women—there's no coz'ning us.

Finis.

Title. Mrs. Knep] *Q 2–5, O;* Mr.   28. thought] *Q 1;* taught *Q 2–5, O.*
Hart *Q 1.*

15. *buckram*] precise, stiff.   22. *Flanders mares*] mistresses.

Appendix

Chronology

Approximate dates are indicated by *.

Political and Literary Events	*Life and Major Works of Wycherley*
1631 John Dryden born.	
1633 Samuel Pepys born.	
1635 Sir George Etherege born.*	
1640 Aphra Behn born.	
1641	Born* at Clive, near Shrewsbury, into a Royalist family of good estate.
1642 First Civil War began (ended 1646). Theaters closed by Parliament. Thomas Shadwell born.*	
1648 Second Civil War.	
1649 Execution of Charles I.	
1650 Jeremy Collier born.	
1651 Hobbes' *Leviathan* published.	
1652 First Dutch War began (ended 1654). Thomas Otway born.	
1653 Nathaniel Lee born.*	

1656
D'Avenant's *THE SIEGE OF RHODES* performed at Rutland House.

At fifteen,* sent to France for his education; associated with the Marquise de Montausier and her *précieux* circle.

1657
John Dennis born.

1658
Death of Oliver Cromwell.
D'Avenant's *THE CRUELTY OF THE SPANIARDS IN PERU* performed at the Cockpit.

1660
Restoration of Charles II.
Theatrical patents granted to Thomas Killigrew and Sir William D'Avenant, authorizing them to form, respectively, the King's and the Duke of York's Companies.

Converted to Catholicism.
Returned to England; entered Queen's College, Oxford, in July.
Reconverted to Church of England.
Entered Inner Temple in November.

1661
Cowley's *THE CUTTER OF COLEMAN STREET*.
D'Avenant's *THE SIEGE OF RHODES* (expanded to two parts).

1662
Charter granted to the Royal Society.

1663
Dryden's *THE WILD GALLANT*.
Tuke's *THE ADVENTURES OF FIVE HOURS*.

1664
Sir John Vanbrugh born.
Dryden's *THE RIVAL LADIES*.
Dryden and Howard's *THE INDIAN QUEEN*.
Etherege's *THE COMICAL REVENGE*.

1665
Second Dutch War began (ended 1667).
Great Plague.

Dryden's *THE INDIAN EM-PEROR*.
Orrery's *MUSTAPHA*.

1666
Fire of London.
Death of James Shirley.

1667
Milton's *Paradise Lost* published.
Sprat's *The History of the Royal Society* published.
Dryden's *SECRET LOVE*.

1668
Death of D'Avenant.
Dryden made Poet Laureate.
Dryden's *An Essay of Dramatic Poesy* published.
Shadwell's *THE SULLEN LOVERS*.

1669
Pepys terminated his diary.
Susannah Centlivre born.

1670
William Congreve born.
Dryden's *THE CONQUEST OF GRANADA*, Part I.

1671
Dorset Garden Theatre (Duke's Company) opened.
Colley Cibber born.
Milton's *Paradise Regained* and *Samson Agonistes* published.
Dryden's *THE CONQUEST OF GRANADA*, Part II.
THE REHEARSAL, by the Duke of Buckingham and others.

Performance (March*) of *LOVE IN A WOOD; OR, ST. JAMES'S PARK*, a comedy which won him the favor of the Duchess of Cleveland, and indirectly of the Duke of Buckingham.

1672
Third Dutch War began (ended 1674).
Joseph Addison born.
Richard Steele born.
Dryden's *MARRIAGE A LA MODE*.

Performance (August*) of *THE GENTLEMAN DANCING-MASTER*, a less successful comedy.

1674
New Drury Lane Theatre (King's Company) opened.
Death of Milton.
Nicholas Rowe born.
Thomas Rymer's *Reflections on Aristotle's Treatise of Poesy* (translation of Rapin) published.

1675
Dryden's *AURENG-ZEBE*.

Performance in January of *THE COUNTRY WIFE*.

1676
Etherege's *THE MAN OF MODE*.
Otway's *DON CARLOS*.
Shadwell's *THE VIRTUOSO*.

Performance in December of *THE PLAIN DEALER*, from whose protagonist he acquired the name of "Manly" Wycherley.

1677
Dryden's *ALL FOR LOVE*.
Lee's *THE RIVAL QUEENS*.
Rymer's *Tragedies of the Last Age Considered* published.

1678
Popish Plot.
George Farquhar born.
Bunyan's *Pilgrim's Progress* (Part I) published.

Illness; visited France for his health, with financial aid from the King.

1679
Exclusion Bill introduced.
Death of Thomas Hobbes.
Death of Roger Boyle, Earl of Orrery.
Charles Johnson born.

1680
Death of Samuel Butler.
Death of John Wilmot, Earl of Rochester.
Dryden's *THE SPANISH FRIAR*.
Lee's *LUCIUS JUNIUS BRUTUS*.
Otway's *THE ORPHAN*.

Secret marriage to the widowed Countess of Drogheda incurred the displeasure of the King, who had offered Wycherley the tutorship of his son, the young Duke of Richmond.

1681
Charles II dissolved Parliament at Oxford.

Death of wife; involved in lawsuits with her family.

Dryden's *Absalom and Achitophel* published.
Tate's adaptation of *KING LEAR*.

1682
The King's and the Duke of York's Companies merged into the United Company.

Put into Fleet Prison for debt.

Dryden's *The Medal, MacFlecknoe,* and *Religio Laici* published.
Otway's *VENICE PRESERVED*.

1683
Rye House Plot.
Death of Thomas Killigrew.

1685
Death of Charles II; accession of James II.
Revocation of the Edict of Nantes.
The Duke of Monmouth's Rebellion.
Death of Otway.
John Gay born.
Crowne's *SIR COURTLY NICE*.
Dryden's *ALBION AND ALBANIUS*.

1686

Freed by James II; given pension of £200.

1687
Death of the Duke of Buckingham.

Reconverted to Catholicism.

Dryden's *The Hind and the Panther* published.
Newton's *Principia* published.

1688
The Revolution.
Alexander Pope born.
Shadwell's *THE SQUIRE OF ALSATIA*.

1689
The War of the League of Augsburg began (ended 1697).

Lost pension after the Revolution.

Toleration Act.

In debt, retired to Clive; a Jacobite.

Death of Aphra Behn.
Shadwell made Poet Laureate.

Dryden's *DON SEBASTIAN*.
Shadwell's *BURY FAIR*.

1690
Battle of the Boyne.
Locke's *Two Treatises of Government*
and *An Essay concerning Human
Understanding* published.

1691
Death of Etherege.
Langbaine's *An Account of the
Dramatic Poets* published.

1692
Death of Lee.
Death of Shadwell.
Tate made Poet Laureate.

1693
George Lillo born.
Rymer's *A Short View of Tragedy*
published.
Congreve's *THE OLD BACHELOR*.

1694
Death of Queen Mary.
Southerne's *THE FATAL
MARRIAGE*.

1695
Group of actors led by Thomas
Betterton leave Drury Lane and
establish a new company at
Lincoln's Inn Fields.
Congreve's *LOVE FOR LOVE*.
Southerne's *OROONOKO*.

1696
Cibber's *LOVE'S LAST SHIFT*.
Vanbrugh's *THE RELAPSE*.

1697
Treaty of Ryswick ended the War
of the League of Augsburg.
Charles Macklin born.
Congreve's *THE MOURNING
BRIDE*.
Vanbrugh's *THE PROVOKED
WIFE*.

Death of litigious father Daniel.
Returned to London.

– 148 –

1698

Collier controversy started with the publication of *A Short View of the Immorality and Profaneness of the English Stage.*

1699

Farquhar's *THE CONSTANT COUPLE.*

1700

Death of Dryden.

Blackmore's *Satire against Wit* published.

Congreve's *THE WAY OF THE WORLD.*

1701

Act of Settlement.

War of the Spanish Succession began (ended 1713).

Death of James II.

Rowe's *TAMERLANE.*

Steele's *THE FUNERAL.*

1702

Death of William III; accession of Anne.

The Daily Courant began publication.

Cibber's *SHE WOULD AND SHE WOULD NOT.*

1703

Death of Samuel Pepys.

Rowe's *THE FAIR PENITENT.*

1704

Capture of Gibraltar; Battle of Blenheim.

Defoe's *The Review* began publication (1704–1713).

Swift's *A Tale of a Tub* and *The Battle of the Books* published.

Cibber's *THE CARELESS HUSBAND.*

Publication of *Miscellany Poems* led to friendship with the young Alexander Pope.

1705

Haymarket Theatre opened.

Steele's *THE TENDER HUSBAND.*

1706
Battle of Ramillies.
Farquhar's *THE RECRUITING OFFICER*.

1707
Union of Scotland and England.
Death of Farquhar.
Henry Fielding born.
Farquhar's *THE BEAUX' STRATAGEM*.

1708
Downes' *Roscius Anglicanus* published.

1709
Samuel Johnson born.
Rowe's edition of Shakespeare published.
The Tatler began publication (1709–1711).
Centlivre's *THE BUSY BODY*.

1711
Shaftesbury's *Characteristics* published.
The Spectator began publication (1711–1712).
Pope's *An Essay on Criticism* published.

1713
Treaty of Utrecht ended the War of the Spanish Succession.
Addison's *CATO*.

1714
Death of Anne; accession of George I.
Steele became Governor of Drury Lane.
John Rich assumed management of Lincoln's Inn Fields.
Centlivre's *THE WONDER: A WOMAN KEEPS A SECRET*.
Rowe's *JANE SHORE*.

1715
Jacobite Rebellion.
Death of Tate.
Rowe made Poet Laureate.

Married to a young woman though
in ill health.
Death on December 31.

1716
Addison's *THE DRUMMER.*

1717
David Garrick born.
Cibber's *THE NON-JUROR.*
Gay, Pope, and Arbuthnot's
*THREE HOURS AFTER MAR-
RIAGE.*

1718
Death of Rowe.
Centlivre's *A BOLD STROKE FOR
A WIFE.*

1719
Death of Addison.
Defoe's *Robinson Crusoe* published.
Young's *BUSIRIS, KING OF
EGYPT.*

1720
South Sea Bubble.
Samuel Foote born.
Steele suspended from the Gover-
norship of Drury Lane (restored
1721).
Steele's *The Theatre* (periodical)
published.
Hughes' *THE SIEGE OF
DAMASCUS.*

1721
Walpole became first Minister.

1722
Steele's *THE CONSCIOUS
LOVERS.*

1723
Death of Susannah Centlivre.
Death of D'Urfey.

1725
Pope's edition of Shakespeare published.

1726
Death of Jeremy Collier.
Death of Vanbrugh.
Law's *Unlawfulness of Stage Entertainments* published.
Swift's *Gulliver's Travels* published.

1727
Death of George I; accession of George II.
Death of Sir Isaac Newton.
Arthur Murphy born.

1728
Pope's *Dunciad* published.
Cibber's *THE PROVOKED HUSBAND* (expansion of Vanbrugh's fragment *A JOURNEY TO LONDON*).
Gay's *THE BEGGAR'S OPERA*.

1729
Goodman's Fields Theatre opened.
Death of Congreve.
Death of Steele.
Edmund Burke born.

1730
Cibber made Poet Laureate.
Oliver Goldsmith born.
Thomson's *The Seasons* published.
Fielding's *THE AUTHOR'S FARCE*.
Fielding's *TOM THUMB* (revised as *THE TRAGEDY OF TRAGEDIES*, 1731).

1731
Death of Defoe.
Lillo's *THE LONDON MERCHANT*.

1732
Covent Garden Theatre opened.
Death of Gay.
George Colman the elder born.
Fielding's *THE COVENT-GARDEN TRAGEDY*.

Fielding's *THE MODERN HUS-BAND*.

Charles Johnson's *CAELIA*.

1733

Pope's *An Essay on Man* published.

1734

Death of Dennis.

The Prompter began publication (1734–1736).

Theobald's edition of Shakespeare published.

Fielding's *DON QUIXOTE IN ENGLAND*.

1736

Fielding led the "Great Mogul's Company of Comedians" at the Little Theatre in the Haymarket (1736–1737).

Fielding's *PASQUIN*.

Lillo's *THE FATAL CURIOSITY*.

1737

The Stage Licensing Act.

Dodsley's *THE KING AND THE MILLER OF MANSFIELD*.

Fielding's *THE HISTORICAL REGISTER FOR* 1736.